D0008237

C. Robert Pace

Measuring Outcomes of College

‹‹‹-‹‹‹-‹‹‹-‹‹‹-‹‹‹-‹‹‹-‹‹‹-‹‹‹-‹‹‹-‹‹‹-‹‹‹-‹‹‹-‹‹‹-‹‹‹-‹‹‹-‹‹‹-‹‹‹-‹‹‹-‹‹‹-

*Fifty Years of Findings
and Recommendations for the Future*

Jossey-Bass Publishers
San Francisco • Washington • London • 1979

MEASURING OUTCOMES OF COLLEGE
Fifty Years of Findings and Recommendations
for the Future
    by C. Robert Pace

Copyright © 1979 by: Jossey-Bass Inc., Publishers
                      433 California Street
                      San Francisco, California 94104
                             &
                      Jossey-Bass Limited
                      28 Banner Street
                      London EC1Y 8QE

Library of Congress Cataloging in Publication Data

Pace, C. Robert, 1912–
  Measuring outcomes of college

  Bibliography: p. 179
  Includes index
  1. Universities and colleges—United States—Evaluation. 2. College
graduates—United States—Evaluation. I. Title.
LB2328.2.P32   378.′98′0973   79-88774
ISBN 0-87589-438-0

Manufactured in the United States of America

JACKET DESIGN BY WILLI BAUM

FIRST EDITION

Code 7940

*The Jossey-Bass Series
in Higher Education*

Contents

The Author

᚛᚛᚛᚛᚛᚛᚛᚛᚛᚛᚛᚛᚛᚛᚛᚛᚛᚛᚛᚛᚛᚛

C. ROBERT PACE is professor of higher education and director of the Laboratory for Research on Higher Education at the University of California, Los Angeles. He was awarded the B.A. degree in English from DePauw University (1933) and the M.A. and Ph.D. degrees in psychology from the University of Minnesota (1935 and 1937, respectively).

Pace has been affiliated with the Commission on Teaching Education of the American Council on Education (1940–1943), the Bureau of Naval Personnel of the Navy Department (1943–1947), and Syracuse University (1947–1961). While at Syracuse, he undertook a variety of tasks, including associate director of its university-wide self-study, director of Evaluation Services Center, special assistant to the chancellor, professor of psychology and education, chairman of the newly formed psychology department, and participant in the creation of a doctoral program in higher education.

Pace has worked on numerous committees, advisory groups, and research projects in higher education—with the American

Council on Education, the College Entrance Examination Board, the Social Science Research Council, the Educational Testing Service, the American College Testing Program, the Fund for the Advancement of Education of the Ford Foundation, the National Institute of Mental Health, the Carnegie Corporation of New York, and the Carnegie Commission on Higher Education.

Since his first book, *They Went to College* (1941)—a follow-up study of former University of Minnesota students—Pace has written more than a dozen books and monographs and more than one hundred journal articles, chapters in books, and other publications—dealing with attitude measurement, evaluation of general education, alumni surveys, testing programs, college environments, college self-studies, college teaching, student learning, and the organization, administration, and curriculum of higher education. For the Carnegie Commission he wrote two books—*Education and Evangelism: A Profile of Protestant Colleges* (1972) and The *Demise of Diversity? A Comparative Profile of Eight Types of Institutions* (1974). For Jossey-Bass he has edited *New Directions for Higher Education: Evaluating Learning and Teaching* (1973).

Measuring Outcomes of College

*Fifty Years of Findings
and Recommendations for the Future*

Prologue

My territory for these essays is this: What do we know about higher education from some fifty or so years of educational testing and surveys? Specifically, what do we know about students' achievement during college—their acquisition of the knowledge, understanding, and intellectual skills that the college curriculum aims to provide? What do we know about achievement after college—the place of college graduates in the world of work, their role as consumers and contributors in civic and cultural affairs, and their judgments about the college experience? And finally, what do we know from surveys about the institutions of higher education—the colleges and universities as organizations and environments?

Clearly, even these more specific questions encompass a vast territory of knowledge. A lot of students have taken a lot of achievement tests over the past forty years. Quite a few colleges have sent questionnaires to their alumni. And all institutions undertake studies of their operations and organization. With a few exceptions, however, I have further limited the territory of these essays by ignoring

1

studies of separate institutions and focusing instead on major surveys involving large numbers of students and alumni and large numbers of institutions. One might suppose that such major inquiries would be familiar to many people, while studies of more limited scope would be unfamiliar. I am not sure why this supposition turns out to be incorrect. Perhaps it is because the results of major surveys tend not to be published as journal articles. By custom, and perhaps by necessity, journal articles are brief—five to twenty pages—and reports of large-scale inquiries do not fit that constricted format. When graduate students and other scholars survey the literature on some topic, they usually examine only the periodical literature, the items appearing in the most relevant journals, and thus this is the literature that gains familiarity. But reports of nationwide testing programs are not found there; they are found in the test manuals and norms published by the testing agencies. Reports of nationwide alumni surveys turn up in books or monographs or chapters in other books or sometimes in government reports. The content is not always evident from the title. Moreover, monographs published thirty or forty years ago are often out of print and the surviving copies can be found only in some university libraries. There is also a tendency, especially among younger scholars, to give their attention primarily to the most recent research and in some cases to assume that what may have been done in the old days is now surely out of date and most likely not worth reading. For all these reasons, the literature reviews most familiar to scholars are typically reviews of journal articles, and these bypass the main subject matter of the essays in the present book. So, my intent is to give some historical perspective to the results of large-scale tests and surveys which have not therefore been assembled with this perspective in mind. As it turns out, this effort seldom overlaps previous reviews.

In 1974, Oscar Lenning, Leo Munday, and others who were then at the American College Testing Program in Iowa City put together a two-volume bibliography of research (Lenning and others, 1974a, 1974b) that had been published during the decade of the 1960s, a bibliography of studies about college students' grades, persistence, learning, and other indicators of success and the personal characteristics associated with college success. In their list of references, they include the names of more than 3,000 authors of research studies, many of whom had produced more than one study; they cite and briefly describe in the text more than 300 studies. But this impressive amount of inquiry, for only a single decade, does not include the results of major nationwide achievement testing programs, or studies of college alumni, or studies of colleges and universities as organizations.

Another major compendium of research (Feldman and Newcomb, 1969a, 1969b) is a two-volume analytical review entitled *The Impact of College on Students*. More than 1,500 empirical studies over a forty-year span from the mid 1920s to the mid 1960s are described and the results classified and summarized. Although by far the most comprehensive and scholarly assessment of the evidence on how colleges have influenced the orientations and characteristics of their students, this review still says little or nothing about students' acquisition of knowledge or about colleges as organizations except as certain features of an institution had an impact on students' development. The key word is *impact*. The authors describe their quest and their analysis in this way: "Under what conditions have what kinds of students changed in what specific ways?" They answer the question by saying "the conditions, it turns out, are very inclusive, ranging from colleges' public images, the characteristics of their students at entrance, the nature of colleges' subenvironments, institutional size, and homogeneity. These and other variables interact with one another in intricate ways. We are now more sure than ever that no simple answers are possible. There are [however] conditions under which colleges have had . . . impacts upon their students, and not least upon students' values. Moreover, the consequences of these impacts often persist after the college years" (1969a, pp. 2–3).

Alexander Astin's research, like many of those studies reviewed by Feldman and Newcomb, has been directed to finding cause and effect relationship. To what extent, in other words, can observed changes in students be attributed to the college experience? Astin (1977) reported the results of several longitudinal studies that he and his associates had conducted between 1965 and 1974, in which college students were reexamined at subsequent dates with respect to a variety of questionnaire items—attitudes and beliefs, self-concept, degree aspirations, extracurricular attainments, persistence in col-

lege, career plans, satisfaction with college, and so on. Altogether
these various studies have involved about 200,000 students from
several hundred colleges and universities, and much of Astin's data
confirms and overlaps in content the inquiries reviewed by Lenning
and Munday and by Feldman and Newcomb. But like their reviews,
Astin's data base does not include students' achievement on standardized or other tests related to the college curriculum.

Another psychologist (Katz, 1976), on the basis of his own
extensive clinical studies and his assessment of other literature related
to students' personal development in college, listed the following
changes as being confirmed by most research: (1) authoritarianism
declines; (2) autonomy grows; (3) self-esteem increases; (4) the
capacity for relatedness becomes enlarged; (5) greater political
sophistication is shown; (6) the conscience is humanized; (7) im-
pulses are expressed more freely; (8) esthetic capacity grows; and
finally, (9) students have a broader grasp of theoretical issues.
Many investigators have also noted an increase in political and social
liberalism and a decrease in formal religious identification and religious activities. This is not to say, of course, that all students change
in these directions. What the research does say is that these are the
characteristic directions of change. Cross-sectional surveys, longitudinal studies, and interview case studies are generally congruent in
their support of such conclusions. Because these aspects of student
growth have been so thoroughly documented, I shall consider them
only briefly in the present essays. Note, however, that Katz's listing
does not directly mention the acquisition of knowledge.

In all this literature, the meaning and relevance of the term
impact is important to understand. One can readily agree with other
researchers that *change* and *impact* have different definitions. When
Feldman and Newcomb say that there are no simple answers to the
questions that have been posed, one needs to remember that the
questions refer to impact. Put another way, they are saying that
there are no simple *explanations* for the changes in attitudes, values,
personal traits, and other characteristics that have been observed.
Perhaps no simple explanations are possible, given the complexity
and interrelatedness of the phenomena. Moreover, researchers themselves have different notions about what constitutes proof: what is
reasonable to one may not be sufficiently rigorous to another.

When researchers write about the *impact* of college on students, they are asking questions about cause and effect. Is the particular behavior or condition they observe really caused by the college? Could it be caused by or attributed to some other event or circumstance—to family background, for example, or I.Q., or simply to the normal process of growing up? We know that students in the twelfth grade are taller and heavier than students in the eighth grade; but we also know that this gain in height and weight was not caused by going to high school. That, of course, is an obvious example of conditions which are associated without having any cause and effect relationship. This association is what statisticians warn of when they remind us that correlation does not prove causation. Naturally, one tries to avoid such patently false conclusions. One way to avoid false conclusions is to be sure that the outcomes or changes one looks for are generally accepted as goals of higher education and that there are events and experiences in college intended to facilitate the attainment of those goals. There is another potential source of false conclusions, however. It is best expressed by the following line of thought: if we can't prove that something is true, it is probably false. More specifically, if our experimental and statistical methods do not find some unique impact of college or of some particular college experience, a result not attributable to any other source, then there has been no impact. All too often the researcher's failure to find a clear cause for change has led the readers of his research report to believe that there has been no change. This is a false reading of the primary evidence. The earth rotates on its axis as it orbits the sun, and no doubt this primary observation would continue to be true whether or not astronomers could explain why. The educational researcher's difficulty in explaining change in no way alters the primary observation that change occurs.

If one asks the question "What?" rather than "Why?", there are a lot of simple answers—clear, straightforward, and consistent over time. Do students learn anything in college? Yes. Do they themselves believe that they have made progress toward such ends as critical thinking, acquiring a body of facts and knowledge of a special field, personal and social development, tolerance, broadened literary acquaintance, and so on? Yes. Do most college graduates find professional, semiprofessional, or managerial jobs? Yes. Is their income, on the average, higher than that of adults who did not graduate from college? Yes. Do they in their communities participate to a greater extent than others in a variety of civic and cultural affairs? Yes. Do college alumni, in retrospect, feel generally satisfied with their college experience? Yes. If they could do it over again, would they? Yes. Have colleges and universities studied themselves as institutions—their administration, organization, finance, the efficiency and effectiveness of their operations and programs? Yes. Do many colleges make such studies of themselves? Yes.

The primary descriptive evidence is strong and consistent. Students change during the college experience; and the status of college graduates is demonstrably different from that of nongraduates in many respects. The focus of this book is on the primary evidence. Moreover, I make no effort to review the literature or update any bibliography with another thousand or so references. Rather, with occasional exceptions, I have drawn the evidence from what I believe to be landmark studies and lines of inquiry, data obtained from large-scale testing programs and surveys, information about thousands of college students and alumni from hundreds of colleges and universities, and surveys of institutions made at different periods of time over the past forty to fifty years.

That colleges are different from one another and that students are different from one another are obvious to any observer. Any analysis of higher education must deal with these differences. What is characteristic of one segment of higher education or of one group of students may not be characteristic of others. At the same time, to understand differences one needs to know what they differ from. My chief concern is not with differences, or diagnoses, or analyses. Rather, my concerns are with the central tendencies, the main line, and with consistencies over time. These are the baselines from which differences derive meaning. Too often, in exploring differences within the system, we have lost sight and sometimes even been unaware of the central tendencies. One purpose of these essays is to turn our sights upon the main line.

I

Achievement During College: Undergraduates

Between their arrival as freshmen and their graduation at the end of the senior year, most college students take thirty to forty-five different courses. The number depends generally on whether the college's calendar is divided into two semesters of fifteen or sixteen weeks each or into three quarters of about eleven weeks each and on the number of units or credits the college allocates to its various courses. In any case, it is surely fair to state that students' performance is judged on at least thirty to forty-five separate occasions during college. More likely, since midterm as well as final examinations are customary, and since some instructors give quizzes even more frequently, most students are tested sixty to ninety times or more. Moreover, because students seldom take more than two or three different courses from the same professor, the judgments of their performance are made by twenty to thirty or more different faculty

7

members. Graduation is contingent on satisfactory performance on all or nearly all of these tests, most of which are created by the instructor who teaches the course. Their aim is to enable the student to demonstrate his or her knowledge and understanding of the subject matter and to give the instructor some reasonable basis for judging whether the student's demonstrated achievement merits a passing grade.

Although the measurement of students' achievement is a universal and frequent occurrence in college, the results are rarely known by or reported to anyone except the individual student, the individual professor, and the registrar who records the grade. In addition, professors rarely give a test at the beginning of a course and the same test at the end so as to determine how much students have gained in their knowledge and understanding of the subject. All that is known from locally constructed final exams is that the student has demonstrated some acceptable grasp of the course material.

Though there have been cases in which the same test has been given at both the beginning and the end of a course, I have never read or heard of an example which showed that students knew less about the subject at the end of the course than they knew at the beginning. However much or little students may learn in the courses they take, and however much or little information they may subsequently retain, they do indeed acquire some knowledge they did not previously possess. Evidence to support a contrary conclusion does not exist. So, any serious discussion of student achievement in college must begin with the basic truth that when students go to college, they do indeed learn something about a great many subjects.

End-of-course achievement tests, prepared by instructors for their own students, are limited to local use. Systematic and comparative documentation of what students have learned requires the use of standardized achievement tests that can be given to many students at disparate colleges. Such tests are constructed by national testing agencies, such as the Educational Testing Service. To understand the evidence from these sources one needs to know about the content of these achievement tests as well as the scope of their use.

The extensive use of objective achievement tests in college is primarily a twentieth-century phenomenon. Indeed, the wide use of so-called objective tests of any sort—tests in which the correct responses or answers can be counted by clerks or by machines—is primarily a twentieth-century development. The first such test applied on a truly massive scale was the Army Alpha, purported to be an intelligence test, given to American soldiers during World War I. During World War II the Army General Classification Test was administered to more than nine million men. The first version of the Scholastic Aptitude Test, still the most widely used test for high school students who are applying for admission to college, was developed by the College Entrance Examination Board in 1926. The Educational Testing Service came into existence in 1948. The American College Testing Program, the only other current and major agency that develops college admissions tests, was founded in 1959. In 1975–76 about a million and a half individuals took the Scholastic Aptitude Test, and another million or so took the test battery developed by the American College Testing Program; about 300,000 individuals took one or more of the College Board's achievement tests for college admission; and about 250,000 students took one or more tests designed for advanced placement in college courses or for obtaining college credit in various subjects. In addition, aptitude or achievement tests for admission to graduate or professional school probably account for another 500,000.

The focus of this chapter is on achievement test results, not on the more widely used aptitude tests such as the verbal and mathematical scores from the Scholastic Aptitude Test or the verbal and quantitative scores from the Graduate Record Examinations. The aptitude tests, of course, can only measure abilities that have been developed through prior learning and are in that sense also basically measures of achievement. Our concern with achievement tests, however, is with ones whose content reflects subject matter commonly encountered in college—that is, with knowledge and understanding in the sciences, the social sciences, the humanities and arts, and with more specific college subjects such as economics, chemistry, and psychology. What do we know about students' achievement from having administered these standardized objective tests to large numbers of students in many colleges and universities? The evidence is found mainly in the test manuals prepared by the testing agencies. Our task then is to examine the different manuals and look at results obtained at different periods of time. Do seniors get higher scores than juniors or sophomores or freshmen? Do student scores increase in relation to the amount of course work they have had in topics most closely related to the test content? Have the results of such comparisons been more or less the same in the 1930s and '40s, the 1950s and '60s, and the 1970s?

The landmark studies or sources of data from achievement tests that I have selected for answering these questions are as follows:

* The Pennsylvania study undertaken during 1928, 1930, and 1932, in which nearly all the college sophomores and seniors in all the colleges of the state were tested.
* The Tests of General Education, produced as part of the Graduate Record Office of the Carnegie Foundation for the Advancement of Teaching, in the 1940s.
* The revised versions of the Graduate Record Examinations' Area Tests and Advanced Tests in the 1950s and 1960s, developed after the Cooperative Test Service and the Graduate Record Examination program became parts of the newly formed Educational Testing Service.
* The College Board's College Level Examination Program (CLEP) in the 1960s and 1970s.
* And the Undergraduate Assessment Program, developed by the Educational Testing Service in the 1970s.

The Pennsylvania Study

No achievement testing program, before or since, has equaled the Pennsylvania study in the sheer volume of knowledge measured by the tests given to college sophomores and seniors. It was a classic study, of epic proportion; and it remains unsurpassed. The monograph (Learned and Wood, 1938) in which the basic results of the testing program are reported is aptly called *The Student and His Knowledge*.

In May 1928, approximately 70 percent of all the college seniors in the state took a battery of achievement tests requiring twelve hours to complete. The tests were given in four sessions of three hours each. The first session tested knowledge about the physical world, including the tools of scientific investigation, and knowledge of physics, chemistry, astronomy, geology, geography, biology, botany, zoology, and physiology. The second session tested knowledge of basic concepts and methods of inquiry in some of the social sciences (psychology, anthropology, and sociology, for instance) as well as statistical concepts, foreign languages (any two from among Greek, Latin, French, German, Italian, and Spanish), and knowledge of ancient cultures (primitive, Near Eastern, Greek, and Roman). The third session assessed knowledge of preindustrial Western civilization (its social, economic, political, intellectual, literary, and artistic attributes). The fourth session covered similar topics with respect to more recent Western civilization, in addition to knowledge about non-Western civilizations (Chinese, Japanese, Indian, and Moslem). Altogether, there were about 3200 test questions—approximately 450 in the sciences; 1150 in languages, literature, and the fine arts; and 1600 in history and the social sciences.

In the spring of 1930 a revised battery of achievement tests was given to college sophomores, and the same test was given to seniors in 1932. The revised tests had the same broad scope and purpose but were reduced in length to eight hours. The foreign language tests were omitted. An English test (vocabulary, spelling, punctuation, grammar, and literature) and a math test (arithmetic to calculus) were added. The English test (450 items) and the math test (210 items took about four hours. The other four hours of testing (1222 items) dealt with what was described as general culture (the sciences, foreign literature, the fine arts, history, and the social sciences).

The early test makers saw as one of the assets of objective test items—true/false, matching, multiple choice—their ability to cover a very large range of information. But the reasons for developing such extensive tests—3200 items in the initial battery and 1882 items in the subsequent one—were more fundamental than simply exploiting the capacity of new-type test items. Underlying these measures was a view of education clearly expressed in the introduction of the report.

Knowledge is the product of thought, and not only or chiefly its raw material. One starts with fresh impressions and

steadily refines their relationships until they harmonize in a
sequence of consistent ideas. The power of organizing ideas or
of reasoning with them is a function of a clear understanding
of the facts themselves in their relationships, and proceeds
from the thinking which establishes that understanding . . .
Thus an item of knowledge called for in the tests is significant
because it bears to other knowledge exact relationships which
only clear thinking can have produced. A correct answer carries
these connections with it. "What is the daily speed of the earth
in its orbit?" One does not learn such things "by heart," but
given the distance from earth to sun, anyone who knows the
relationship of a diameter to a circumference and can divide a
year into days can approximate the true answer at once. Such
knowledge lasts because it has relationships of which one is
aware and apart from which it would disappear. The awareness of the relationships which the item sustains is thinking,
and producing that awareness is education. The belief that
enduring knowledge possesses just this significance, that it is
the outcome of education and not merely its starting point,
will explain why the present study has sought to focus its
knowledge tests altogether on mental possessions of this
nature. . . . To deserve recognition, knowledge must be a
relatively permanent and available equipment of the student
[and] it must be so familiar and so sharply defined that it comes
freely to mind when needed. . . . It is assumed that the
specific aim of formal education should be . . . to produce
matured knowledge in the student. . . . [Moreover] a student's knowledge when used as adequate evidence of education . . . should represent as nearly as possible the complete
individual . . . a coherent intellectual physiognomy. . . . If
the examinations used in this undertaking have verged upon
the panoramic and have sought to reflect the largest possible
areas for recognition in the fields presented, this has been done
not as a casual *tour de force,* but in the belief that school or
teacher can be most helpful to a growing mind only when the
full scope and variety of its activities are understood and related [Learned and Wood, 1938, pp. 6–10].

This philosophy of education and of measurement was further
expressed in an announcement issued in advance to each student
who took the first set of tests in 1928—an announcement that in-

cluded an explanatory outline of the examination, sample test questions, and the following points, among others:

> The purpose underlying the proposed test is to learn what the bachelor's degree . . . amounts to in terms, first, of clear, available, important ideas, and second, of ability to discriminate exactly among ideas and to use them accurately in thinking. These objects are among the main reasons for acquiring an education and for the existence of educational institutions.
>
> The questions, instead of requiring written answers, will be of a sort to test memory, judgment, and reasoning ability through simple recognition. . . . By this method a large amount of ground can be covered in a short time.
>
> The test has been organized in a manner that presents knowledge in certain definite relationships. Taken as a whole it might serve as a general scheme for a liberal education. The topics often cut across courses as given in college; nevertheless . . . the subjects that you have studied will all be found in their appropriate location.
>
> Owing to the comprehensive nature of the examination, no one student will be able to answer more than a small proportion of all the questions presented. He will find these scattered throughout the papers, very numerous at certain points and very rare at others. He should therefore be on his guard against discouragement, and should bear in mind that all students in the state who are taking the test are in the same position. His object should be to cover the ground completely and to respond at all points where the answer comes promptly and clearly to his mind [pp. 371–372].

Approximately 4,500 graduating seniors from forty-five Pennsylvania colleges took this twelve-hour achievement test battery. The test makers were right when they said that no one student would be able to answer correctly more than a small proportion of all the questions presented. The highest score of any student tested was 1,560 out of the 3,200 items in the test. The average score of all seniors in the state was 570. There were also 194 faculty members from fifteen institutions who took these tests. The highest faculty score was 2260; the average, 920.

The report of the Pennsylvania study emphasizes mainly the range of scores made by students in each of the forty-five colleges, the great overlap in the distributions of scores between institutions, and the differences in average scores between the different institutions. The lowest scores of students at some colleges were higher than the highest scores at others. In 1928 not many high school graduates went to college—probably fewer than one in ten. Yet even among this restricted group the differences in "intelligence" were great, and the differences in achievement were as great or greater. There was not then, nor is there today, any defined minimum amount of knowledge constituting a baccalaureate degree.

My concern, however, is not with these well-documented facts of individual differences and diversity; rather it is with the evidence that knowledge is related to what one has studied and that the more extensively one has studied in any general field, the more one knows about it. For this purpose the scores of students on three major parts of the test are presented: (1) natural sciences, (2)' language, literature, and fine arts, and (3) social studies. These three part scores cover the bulk of the examination.

Is there a relationship between the amount of course work students have had in each of these broad fields and their scores on that part of the test? Yes. The next three tables show these results.

Table 1, on natural science, shows that for all the college seniors in the state who had no more than six credit hours of work in the natural sciences, the average score was 46, whereas the average score for all the seniors who had fifty-five or more credit hours of work in the natural sciences was 120. With each increment in the number of credit hours there is a roughly corresponding increment in the average test score. The righthand column shows the average scores of students, statewide, who had the greatest number of their credit hours in particular academic fields, these being the fields with the largest number of students—two representing natural science (chemistry and engineering), two representing language and fine arts (English and French), and two representing social studies (history and economics). The report does not indicate how many credit hours in the field these students had; it simply states that they received more credit hours in that field than in any other. Clearly, students who took a lot of chemistry or engineering courses made relatively high scores on the natural science part of the test. The

Table 1. Test Scores and Credit Hours in Natural Sciences

Credit Hours	Average Scores	Change Between Scores	Average Scores of Students Specializing in Six Popular Fields
55 or more	120	+ 9	Chemistry: 129 Engineering: 114
49–54	110	+10	
43–48	101		
		+10	
37–42	91		
		+13	
31–36	78		
		+ 4	
25–30	74		
		+ 8	
19–24	66		English: 65
		+ 5	Economics: 64
13–18	61		History: 60
		+ 6	French: 58
7–12	55		
		+ 9	
0– 6	46		

Source: Learned and Wood, 1938, p. 118; adapted from Chart 16.

statewide average score in natural science was 78 (out of 450); and the statewide average number of credit hours in natural science was 37.

Table 2 shows the results for language, literature, and fine arts. With one small exception, the scores and credit hours increase together, as they did in Table 1, but the increments are much more irregular. As one might expect, students who had the largest number of their credits in French or English made relatively high scores on this part of the test. The statewide average score in language, literature, and fine arts was 168; and the statewide average number of credit hours in those fields was 42.

Table 3, showing the corresponding results for social studies, does not have the same parallel progression of credit hours and scores that was so clear in the two other tables. Although there is a substantial difference between the bottom and the top of the ladder, the upward climb is irregular. As was true for the other parts of the test, however, the scores of students who had the largest number of their

Table 2. Test Scores and Credit Hours in Language, Literature, and Fine Arts

Credit Hours	Average Scores	Change Between Scores	Average Scores of Students Specializing in Six Popular Fields
73–78	250		
		+14	
67–72	236		
		+ 4	
61–66	232		French: 231
		+29	English: 216
55–60	203		
		+ 2	
49–54	201		
		+13	
43–48	188		
		+25	History: 168
37–42	163		
		+12	
31–36	151		Chemistry: 150
		+ 9	
25–30	142		Economics: 143
		+15	
19–24	127		
		+19	Engineering: 119
13–18	108		
		− 3	
7–12	111		

Source: Learned and Wood, 1938, p. 119; adapted from Chart 17.

college credits in the category being tested (history or economics, in this case) were relatively high. The statewide average score in social studies was 241; and the statewide average number of credit hours in social studies was 52.

The authors of the Pennsylvania report have this to say about why the pattern of results in social studies differs from the results on the two other parts of the test:

> The material of natural science curricula is in great part sequential. Advanced courses rest more or less securely on elementary ideas that must be constantly reviewed and kept fresh. . . . Similarly, in the language, literature, and fine arts section of the examination, the dominant factor contributing nearly one-half of the average score was language, which is likewise a field in which knowledge is sequential; time and the

Table 3. Test Scores and Credit Hours in Social Studies

Credit Hours	Average Scores	Change Between Scores	Average Scores of Students Specializing in Six Popular Fields
97–108	292		
		+32	History: 279
85–96	260		Economics: 271
		− 2	
73–84	262		
		+ 9	
61–72	253		
		+ 7	
49–60	246		English: 246
		+16	
37–48	230		
		− 2	
25–36	232		
		− 2	
13–24	234		Chemistry: 222
		+38	Engineering: 217
1–12	196		French: 216

Source: Learned and Wood, 1938, p. 120; adapted from Chart 18.

cumulative effect of practice are essential. Social studies, on the contrary, are made up of material that does not necessarily cohere. History, economics, government, sociology, education— these are all fields in which course after course may single out certain groups of ideas without either presupposing or preparing the way for ideas contained in any other course [p. 122].

Overall, the senior survey results can be summarized quite simply. With respect to each of the three part scores of the test, all groups of students who had less than the statewide average number of related credit hours had average test scores that were also below the statewide average score; and all groups of students who had more than the statewide average number of related credit hours also had average test scores that were higher than the statewide average score. In the natural science section of the test, the average score of those who had the most credit hours was 2-1/2 times greater than the average score of those who had the least number of credit hours. In language, literature, and fine arts the magnitude of the difference was 2-1/3 times; and it was 1-1/2 times in social studies.

Conclusion: Students learn what they study, and the more they study, the more they learn.

The next phase of the Pennsylvania study consisted of testing sophomores in 1930 and seniors in 1932. The results are shown in Table 4. On the left side of the table are the mean scores for all sophomores tested in 1930 and all seniors tested in 1932. Not only on the total test of 1,882 items but on each part of the test, the average scores of seniors are higher than the average scores of sophomores. On the right side of the table are the average scores of the same students in the same colleges tested first when they were sophomores and then again when they were seniors. The results from this longitudinal comparison are very similar to the results from the cross-sectional comparison, despite the fact that half of those tested as sophomores were no longer in school two years later and that the number of seniors in the longitudinal comparison was nearly one fourth less than the total number of seniors. The sophomores who subsequently became seniors were, of course, a more select group than the total population of sophomores. This is reflected in their higher scores on all parts of the test, not only when they were sophomores but also when they were seniors. Nevertheless, the relative gains of this longitudinal group are about the same as the differences between the two groups in the cross-sectional comparison. For example, on the general culture test, the mean score (325) of the senior group is 25 percent higher (an inferred gain) than the mean score (260) of the sophomore group. But if one compares only the same students' scores at two points in time (281 and 337), the actual gain is 20 percent. By looking only at longitudinal data one underestimates the real differences that exist between the total group of sophomores and the total group of seniors. By looking only at cross-sectional comparisons one overestimates the actual gains that occur. In any case, the conclusions from the Pennsylvania data are obvious: seniors know more than they knew when they were sophomores; seniors as a group know more than sophomores as a group.

The amount of gain from the end of the sophomore year to the end of the senior year—up 1 percent in math, up 10 percent in English, up 13 percent in sciences, up 20 percent in fine arts, up 25 percent in history and social studies, and up 26 percent in foreign literature—may strike some readers as rather modest, not much to

Table 4. Achievement Test Scores of Pennsylvania Sophomores in 1930 and Seniors in 1932

Number of Items	Subject	All Sophomores[a]	All Seniors[a]	Difference	Same Students[b] As Sophomores	As Seniors	Difference
450	English	194	215	+25	205	226	+21
210	Math	71	77	+ 6	77	78	+ 1
292	Science	90	103	+13	92	104	+12
333	Foreign Literature	52	68	+16	57	72	+15
251	Fine Arts	50	62	+12	54	65	+11
346	History & Social Studies	70	93	+23	77	96	+19
1222	Total General Culture	260	325	+65	281	337	+56
1882	Total All Tests	526	620	+94	562	642	+80

[a] 5691 sophomores from forty-six colleges; 3704 seniors from forty-five colleges.
[b] 2830 sophomores who became seniors, from forty-five colleges.
Source: Learned and Wood, 1938, pp. 380–382; composite adapted from the Appendix, Tables 3, 4, and 6.

show, really, for two more years of college work. But one needs to remember that the student's major field of study during the last two years of college touches only a small part of the total content of these achievement tests. Very few students take any math courses beyond the freshman or sophomore year unless they are majoring in math or in a field where advanced math is required, such as physics or engineering. Very few students take any science courses beyond the introductory level if they are majoring in English, or history, or fine arts, or French. In fact, one might reasonably expect considerable forgetting to occur, but it doesn't.

In every one of the forty-five colleges the mean score of seniors on the total test was higher than the mean score of those same students when they were sophomores. We can also examine the changes in scores on each part of the test. For this purpose the following six part scores were used—math, science, fine arts, foreign literature, English literature, and history and social studies. In fifteen of the forty-five colleges there was an increase in the mean score on every section of the test except mathematics. The direction of change, for each part of the test at each college, is listed below.

Total test	up in all 45 colleges
General culture	up in all 45 colleges
Foreign literature	up in 43 colleges, down in 2
History and social studies	up in 43 colleges, down in 2
English literature	up in 39 colleges, down in 6
Science	up in 39 colleges, down in 6
Fine arts	up in 36 colleges, down in 9
Math	up in 21 colleges, down in 24

By grouping all the seniors from all 45 colleges according to their major field of study as upperclassmen, we can see the progress of these different major groups, as follows:

- Engineering majors made gains on all parts of the test.
- Chemistry and physics majors made gains on all parts of the test.
- Natural science majors made gains on all parts of the test.
- Math majors made gains on all parts of the test.
- Modern language majors made gains on all parts of the test except mathematics.

- English majors made gains on all parts of the test except mathematics.
- History majors made gains on all parts of the test except mathematics.
- Social studies majors (excluding history) made gains on all parts of the test except mathematics.

The gain in the mean score was, of course, greatest on the parts of the test most closely related to the student's major. For the test as a whole, the gains were typically a little more than one third of a standard deviation (.39); on those parts of the test most closely related to the student's major, the typical gain was a little more than two thirds of a standard deviation (.69).

Conclusion: During the last two years of college the typical student in the Pennsylvania study gained significantly in the general knowledge measured by these achievement tests, also gained in all or nearly all the specific subjects measured by the tests (except mathematics) regardless of the major field of study, and gained most on those parts of the test which were most clearly related to the major field.

Tests of General Education

Following the Pennsylvania study, there were two achievement test programs which had rather wide currency: the General Culture Tests produced by the Cooperative Test Service, and the Tests of General Education of the Graduate Record Office. Of these two, the Tests of General Education were most like the ones used in the Pennsylvania study, both in style and content. The total battery of exams required eight hours and included the following topics: general mathematics, physical sciences, biological sciences, social studies, literature, arts, effectiveness of expression, and vocabulary. Except for the vocabulary test, the topics are clearly related to the subject matter of the college curriculum.

The results from these tests, as indeed from most tests subsequently discussed in this chapter, are reported on a standard scale rather than as direct raw scores indicating how many items a student answered correctly. The standard scale has been commonly defined as having a mean or average of 500 and a standard deviation of 100, based on the performance of a normative or baseline group of students for whom the test was intended. One standard deviation from the mean, plus and minus, includes two thirds of the scores. Thus, a score of 600 or higher would be attained by only one sixth or fewer of the students and a score of 400 or lower would be attained by only one sixth or fewer of the students. A simpler way to interpret these standard score scales is to translate them into percentiles, or the percentage of students scoring above and below any given level. A standard score of 500 means that 50 percent of the students scored lower than that; a standard score of 550 means that 69 percent scored lower than that; and a standard score of 600 means that 84 percent scored lower than that, or, turning it around, that only 16 percent scored higher than 600. We do not really know how much of an increase of knowledge is expressed by these differences in relative standing. However, we do know that according to the common practice in constructing standardized achievement tests, the average or middle score typically means that approximately half the items (usually a little more) have been answered correctly. Obviously, higher scores mean that a greater percentage of the items have been answered correctly. If the highest score in the standardization group means that the student responded to all or very nearly all the items correctly, then perhaps the various percentile positions along the way correspond roughly to the percentage of items in the test that were correctly answered. However, percentages and percentiles have different meanings. Percentages are equal intervals along a linear scale. Percentiles are positions along a normal distribution of scores. What this means is that in the middle range of scores, a small increase in the percentage of items answered correctly will produce a larger increase in the percentile ranking attached to the score; and at the higher and lower ranges of scores, a larger increase in the percentage of items answered correctly is necessary to produce a similar increase in the percentile ranking. These are general guidelines for interpreting standard scores and the differences between them.

The first set of results from the Tests of General Education, comparing the scores of slightly more than 1000 students from sixteen colleges as sophomores in 1946 and again as seniors in 1948, is shown in Table 5. The mean scores of seniors, on all parts of the test,

Table 5. Tests of General Education: 1,012 Students from Sixteen Colleges Tested in 1946 as Sophomores and again in 1948 as Seniors

Test	Sophomores	Seniors	Gain		
Mathematics	466	497	+31		+42
Physical science	477	484	+ 7	Gains for natural science majors	+27
Biological science	476	507	+31		+60
Social studies	445	498	+53	Gains for social studies majors	+59
Literature	476	507	+31		+38
Arts	479	505	+26	Gains for humanities majors	+29
Effectiveness of expression	482	517	+35		+40
Average	471	502	+31		

Source: Lannholm, 1952.

are always higher than the mean scores of those same students when they were sophomores. The size of the difference is typically about one third of a standard deviation. Given the average starting and ending scores, this represents a gain from the 38th percentile to the 50th percentile. The figures at the right of the table indicate that the gains of students on those parts of the test most clearly related to their own major field of study are noticeably greater than the gains for students in general. These differences or gains are largest in the fields of science and mathematics; and these fields are the ones most specialized in their content. Moreover, few social studies or human- ities majors take courses in science or math during their last two years of college, whereas many math and science majors take at least some courses in social sciences or humanities in their junior or senior year. Generally, these results of testing in 1946–1948 confirm the two basic conclusions I drew from the Pennsylvania data in 1930–1932: first, seniors know more than they knew when they were sopho- mores; and second, students make their greatest gains on those parts of the test that measure knowledge related to their major field of study.

Graduate Record Examinations:
Area Tests and Advanced Tests

The Area Tests of the Graduate Record Examinations (GRE), introduced in 1954, represent the beginning of a new generation of achievement tests. The Pennsylvania tests and the Tests of General Education emphasized the measurement of knowl- edge and the recall of information (often quite specific to a given subject matter), while not ignoring the students' ability to see rela- tionships between different pieces of knowledge or their awareness of generalizations and principles. As we have seen, the tests were long and provided scores in specific fields of knowledge—The Area Tests, in contrast, are much shorter (three and three-fourths hours), and the subject matter is organized in three very broad categories— social sciences, natural sciences, and humanities. Moreover, the na- ture of the test items is different: whereas the earlier tests measured the students' possession of knowledge in the field, the Area Tests eval- uate students' ability to read, understand, and interpret knowledge.

Of course, the possession of knowledge is implicit in the ability to interpret it; but in this case the requisite knowledge is often given to the students within the test items, and they are then required only to draw appropriate generalizations from it. Whether this change in emphasis has been, on balance, desirable or undesirable is debatable. On the one hand, the newer tests are not as directly related to the specific subject matter of various college courses and are therefore less useful for measuring the amount of knowledge the student acquired from the courses. On the other hand, the newer tests, by emphasizing understanding and interpretation, are probably measuring more significant and more nearly permanent outcomes of education and, because of their generality for a broad field of knowledge, are perhaps more widely applicable to different students from different colleges.

For the Area Tests, I could not locate any longitudinal data covering many students at many different colleges. There are a few examples of before-and-after testing at a single college, but these single examples are not reported here. In one report, the scores of 3,035 seniors from many different colleges were grouped according to the student's major field of study. These results, in Table 6, confirm with data from the 1950s what had previously been shown with data from the 1930s and the 1940s. Natural science majors make the highest scores on the natural science test; humanities majors make the highest scores on the humanities test; and social science majors make the highest scores on the social science test. The differences are especially large in the natural sciences, substantial in the humanities, and small but in the expected direction in the social sciences. These results simply say that students know most what they study most.

Table 6. Graduate Record Examinations: Area Test Scores of 3035 Seniors in 1953–54 in Different Major Fields of Study

	Social Science Test	Humanities Test	Natural Science Test
Social science majors	497	479	455
Humanities majors	481	537	499
Natural science majors	485	478	573

Source: Educational Testing Service, 1954; adapted from Table 12, p. 29.

Table 7. Graduate Record Examinations: Advanced Test Scores of 283 Students Given the Same Test Twice

Test	Juniors	Seniors	Gain	
Advanced psychology test	414	510	+ 96	(105 psychology majors from 10 colleges)
Advanced economics test	413	495	+ 82	(80 economics majors from 8 colleges)
Advanced chemistry test	415	520	+105	(106 chemistry majors from 11 colleges)
Average	414	508		

Note: The tests were given at the beginning of the junior year and at the end of the senior year.
Source: Harvey and Lannholm, 1960; adapted from Tables 1, 2, and 3, pp. 4–6.

The other part of the Graduate Record Examinations program consists of Advanced Tests, subject-matter achievement tests in specific major fields. They are intended for college seniors who are applying for admission to graduate school, and the test content is therefore pitched at a fairly high level. Some longitudinal results from three of these Advanced Tests are shown in Table 7. Although the number of students and institutions in this example is quite small —fewer than 300 upperclassmen at 29 institutions—the table depicts the only instances I could find in which the same test was given to the same students on two different occasions. The scores of the juniors reflect their knowledge of the subject before they had taken any upper-division or advanced courses in it. The scores of these same students as seniors reflect their level of knowledge after taking many advanced courses. Clearly, the differences are substantial —typically close to a full standard deviation, or in these cases, a jump from about the 19th or 20th percentile to the 48th or 58th percentile. Conclusion: Whatever field the students major in (from these three examples), they know a great deal more about it at the end than they knew at the beginning.

The College Level Examination Program (CLEP)

Since the 1960s tests have been developed for the purpose of giving students college credit for knowledge they might have acquired out of college. A program similar in intent existed after World War II whereby servicemen could apply for college credit by examination. To provide a baseline or comparison group against which the colleges themselves could decide whether and how much college credit to allot, the tests were given to a national sample of college sophomores. One set of data from the booklet describing these tests and their use and interpretation is reported here because it again reinforces an earlier conclusion—namely, that the level of students' performance is related to the number of courses they have had. The results in Table 8 show that with each increase in the number of relevant courses, from none, to one, to several, there is a corresponding increase in the mean score on the test.

The next set of data, Table 9, classifies by educational level (highest grade completed) the scores of about 39,000 people who

Table 8. Scale Scores of Sophomores on the General Examinations of the
College Level Examination Program, 1963

	Humanities	History and Social Sciences	Science	Math
Most courses	524	528	549	577
At least one course	498	486	486	497
No courses	439	483	443	445

Note: These results are drawn from a group of approximately 2600 sophomores
at 180 colleges.
Source: Haven, 1964; adapted from Tables C-11, C-12, C-13, and C-14, pp.
56–59.

Table 9. Scores of a USAFI Sample on the CLEP
General Examination, 1965–1966

Highest Grade Completed	Humanities	History and Social Sciences	Sciences	Math	English Composition
15 (N = 1,000)	492	522	537	530	479
14 (N = 3,000)	470	498	517	512	460
13 (N = 5,000)	458	483	502	493	451
12 (N = 30,000)	415	429	447	430	396

Note: Results based on approximately 39,000 individuals.
Source: College Entrance Examination Board, 1968; adapted from Tables II,
III, IV, and V; pp. 8–11.

took the CLEP general examination through the United States
Armed Forces Institute (USAFI). Though there is an obvious
element of selectivity in these results, the differences in the mean
scores of people who had completed the twelfth grade and those
who had completed one or more years of college are very large, and
they increase consistently with each increase in educational level.
Moreover, those high school graduates who took the tests were
planning to attend college and seeking college credit for their
demonstrated competence—that is, they were not "average" high
school graduates.

The Undergraduate Assessment Program:
Area Tests and Field Tests

The Undergraduate Assessment Program (UAP), growing
out of the former Undergraduate Program for Counseling and

Evaluation and the old GRE Institutional Testing Program of the 1960s, is related to the Graduate Record Examinations. The Area Tests of the UAP are fundamentally the same as the Area Tests of the GRE, and the Field Tests of the UAP are similar to the Advanced Tests of the GRE.

As part of the standardization program for the UAP Area Tests, they were administered to about 47,000 college seniors from 211 colleges in the years 1969 to 1971. The colleges were invited to give the same tests to samples of other classes. Most of them did not. The results for all classes are listed in Table 10. Because the samples, both of students and of institutions, are so different in size, one cannot comment with any assurance about the meaning of differences between the classes. In fact, all the differences shown in the table may be meaningless because of the noncomparability of the samples. I have reported the results, nonetheless, partly to illustrate the hazard of interpreting cross-sectional results when the various cross-sections are from different institutions, and partly to note in passing that even with these distortions the scores of the seniors are about half a standard deviation higher than the scores of freshmen. If, as may well have been the case, the institutions that gave the tests to more than one class were a more selective group of institutions, then the mean scores of freshman, sophomores, and juniors shown in the table are higher than the scores of a more representative group would have been.

Somewhat more meaningful comparisons based on the results of these UAP Area Tests are shown in Table 11. Although any interpretation of the differences between sophomores and seniors

Table 10. Undergraduate Assessment Program Area Test Scores

	Humanities	Natural Science	Social Science
Seniors	470	480	446
Juniors	473	490	446
Sophomores	459	471	414
Freshmen	421	434	389

Note: N = Approximately 47,000 seniors from 211 colleges; 5,000 juniors from 111 colleges; 11,000 sophomores from 72 colleges; and 1,500 freshmen from 22 colleges.
Source: Educational Testing Service, 1976; adapted from Tables 26–31; pp. 35–37.

is subject to the same hazard just noted, the hazard is lessened by the fact that at least a third of the institutions are the same. More pertinent, however, is a conclusion one can properly draw by comparing Tables 10 and 11. In Table 11, seniors whose area of interest was the humanities had a mean score of 525 on the humanities test, compared with a mean score of 470, in Table 10, for the total group of seniors from those same colleges. Roughly the same magnitude of difference, about half a standard deviation, is evident for sophomores as well as for seniors, and for the natural science test as well as for the humanities test. When the test is in the student's "area of interest," the scores on it are substantially higher than the scores of the total group of students at the same schools. The total group includes the "interest" group, and because of that overlap in membership, the actual difference between the "area of interest" scores and their opposites (the scores of those whose "interest" is outside the testing area) would be considerably larger. On the social studies test, the "interest" group includes more than half the total group (N=28,000 seniors in Table 11, compared with the total of 47,000 seniors in Table 10, for example), so that the differences between "interest group" and total group are necessarily almost impossible to be revealed.

Another bit of data from the Undergraduate Assessment Program relates to the scores of seniors in specific fields. The norm booklet for these tests has a number of comparisons between the scores

Table 11. UAP Area Test Scores (from the 1969–1971 testing program) Related to Students' "Area of Interest"

	Humanities Test (area of interest in humanities)[a]	Natural Science Test (area of interest in biological science)[b]	(area of interest in physical science)[c]	Social Science Test (area of interest in the social sciences)[d]
Seniors	525	537	556	448
Sophomores	506	510	523	414

[a] N = 10,000 seniors from 190 colleges; 2,300 sophomores from 64 colleges.
[b] N = 6,000 seniors from 160 colleges; 1,600 sophomores from 56 colleges.
[c] N = 3,400 seniors from 150 colleges; 8,500 sophomores from 50 colleges.
[d] N = 28,000 seniors from 181 colleges; 6,000 sophomores from 63 colleges.
Source: Educational Testing Service, 1976; adapted from Tables 26–31; pp. 35–37.

of seniors who had fewer than eight courses in the subject and those
who had eight or more courses. Without exception, the mean scores
of students who had the greater number of courses are higher (see
Table 12). Although the score differences are not large, typically
about one fourth to one third of a standard deviation on the test,
neither are the differences between "fewer than eight" and "eight
or more." There might, for example, be many students in one group
who had only eight or nine. Moreover, it is very likely that all the
students in the "fewer than eight" group had at least five or six
courses, because they would not have taken the test unless the subject was their major field. In short, these results again illustrate the
simple fact that the more one studies a subject, the more one knows
about it.

In the late 1970s, Educational Testing Service made a few
revisions in the Area Tests of its Undergraduate Assessment Program
and published a new Guide (1978). Data in the new Guide come
from approximately 16,000 seniors in 105 colleges, 2200 juniors in
57 colleges, 4200 sophomores in 46 colleges, and 2800 freshmen in
30 colleges, who took the tests in connection with a new norming
program in 1976 to 1978. The pattern of results is basically the same
as the pattern reported for the earlier 1969–1971 testing. On the

**Table 12. Scale Scores of Seniors on the Field Tests of the Undergraduate
Assessment Program, 1969–1971**

	Fewer than Eight Courses	Eight or More Courses	Difference
Biology	539	566	+27
Chemistry	510	539	+29
Engineering	506	528	+22
Economics	483	512	+29
Political science	446	463	+17
Psychology	447	480	+33
Sociology	415	431	+16
History	468	491	+23
Literature	455	491	+36
Philosophy	514	551	+37
French	448	486	+38

Note: The number of students tested varies by major field, ranging from approximately 1,000 to 8,000.
Source: Educational Testing Service, 1976, adapted from Tables 2, 4, 6, 8, 9,
13, 14, 17, 20, 21, and 23; pp. 23–33.

humanities test, the mean score of freshmen was 380; sophomores, 420; juniors, 420; seniors, 446; and seniors who majored in humanities, 492. On the physical sciences test, the mean score of freshmen was 412; sophomores, 455; juniors, 458; seniors, 486; and seniors who majored in physical sciences, 569. On the social sciences test, the mean score of freshmen was 343; sophomores, 383; juniors, 396; and seniors; 422; and for seniors who majored in social sciences the mean score was also 422. No explanation or speculation is given in the Guide about why the mean score of seniors who had majored in the social sciences was no higher than the mean score of seniors in general. In any case, the interpretation of these scores as evidence of gain is hazardous for the same reasons I noted when discussing the 1969–71 data: the samples are different and they do not come from the same colleges. Nevertheless, the differences between freshmen or sophomores, on the one hand, and seniors, on the other hand, are in all instances substantial; and these differences are completely consistent with every other testing program whose results I have reported.

The new UAP Guide also gives results on the Field Tests, comparing the mean scores of majors who had taken "fewer than nine courses" and those who had taken "at least nine courses." Again, the new results are consistent with the previous results. Students who had taken nine or more courses in their major field knew more than students who had taken fewer than nine courses. The differences in mean scores are typically about one fourth of the standard deviation on the scale.

The 1970s

From the use of achievement tests produced by the major testing agencies, little new has been added in the 1970s to our knowledge of college students' achievement. There are, however, two developments under way, each representing a new direction in the measurement of achievement—one at the American College Testing Program and the other at Educational Testing Service.

The College Outcome Measures Project (COMP) is under the direction of Aubrey Forrest at the American College Testing Program in Iowa City. Unlike most achievement tests, which derive their content from the major academic disciplines or from broad areas in the general education curriculum, the ACT project is aimed at measuring the application of facts and concepts and skills believed to be needed for effective functioning as adults. The content of the test relates to three areas of adult activity: functioning within social institutions, using science and technology, and using the arts. Within each of these areas, three types of skills or competence are measured: communicating, solving problems, and clarifying values. For example, the adult domain of functioning within social institutions is measured by items which consider communicating about social institutions, solving social problems, and clarifying social values. Beyond this somewhat unusual design for the test content, COMP differs from other achievement tests in the nature of the stimulus material and in the form of the responses that students make to the material, both of these departures illustrating the realistic or practical intentions of the test makers. The stimulus materials include film excerpts, a taped discussion, a taped newscast, an advertisement, art prints, photographs, recordings of music, graphs and tables, stories, magazine and newspaper articles, and similar realistic material one might encounter in adult life. In responding to most of these materials, students are required to provide their own answers rather than choose among answers supplied to them. In one situation, for example, the student acts as chairperson of an art committee which has recommended the purchase of two paintings for the new library in a rural town. The paintings are on display. The student is told to anticipate that there will be questions from the audience, such as Why are these paintings appropriate for our library? What do the paintings mean? Why are these paintings better than others? Then, the student is given a microphone, questions are asked, and the student's responses are recorded on tape. In another situation the student is required to write a memo intended to persuade someone to take a particular course of action. Both the stimulus materials and the forms of response are in this sense realistic.

Obviously this mode of testing takes a lot of time—time to view, listen, or read the test materials and time to write out or to give an oral response. Field trials of this Measurement Battery in 1977 required about six hours. Moreover, since the responses cannot be read by a machine, additional hours are required for trained judges (presumably faculty members) to rate the adequacy of the students' replies. The COMP annual report for 1978 (Forrest and Steele, 1978) states that it takes about one hour per student to evaluate the written and oral responses; and more than one judge or rater is needed to assure consistency and reliability in the evaluations. The report also indicates that standardized rating scales have been developed to enable faculty members to make reliable judgments.

The overall COMP includes two additional elements. Perhaps in recognition of the time-consuming nature of the Measurement Battery, the authors have also devised an Objective Test format. The same stimulus materials are read, but the students' responses to the various materials consist in choosing, from among four options, two which they regard as good answers. The time required to take this Objective Test version is about two and a half hours and the responses can be scored by machine. The other element in the overall project is called an Activity Inventory. It is not an achievement test. It asks respondents to think about a variety of activities they may have participated in during their lifetime. The activities are grouped in the same six categories that compose the Measurement Battery, with nine examples or topics in each of the six areas. For each topic, there are five levels of participation, ranging from high to low; and the respondent checks the highest level he or she has reached in any activity that was not part of any school or college course. For example, activities involving skill in getting along with people range in level from serving as a leader, spokesperson, or chairperson of a group to participating in organizations or activities that involve little interaction with other members. The Activity Inventory supplements the Measurement Battery or Objective Test by adding an experience factor to the assessment of effective functioning in adult society.

A quite different direction in achievement testing related to general education is illustrated by the recent work of Jonathan Warren at the Berkeley office of the Educational Testing Service. Unlike the ACT project, which focuses on the demonstration of knowledge and competence in a variety of realistic adult applications, the ETS project focuses on the measurement of basic intellectual processes—academic abilities or competences that are acquired

or developed in college and that are of general import beyond the
content or experiences of particular courses. In the report of this
work, the following competences are listed and described (Warren,
1978, p. 13):

- *Communication:* Clarity and precision of written expression;
  ready movement from one mode of written expression to another.
- *Analytic thinking:* Identification of the essential components of
  ideas, of inconsistencies and inaccuracies in the statement of ideas;
  discrimination of fact from conjecture, the important from the
  unimportant, relevant from the irrelevant.
- *Synthesizing ability:* Generalization of ideas to new or broader
  contexts; integration of given knowledge or information into
  more general structures.
- *Awareness:* Sensitivity to the implications of thoughts and actions
  for the social good, and to the importance of values and cultural
  contexts in human affairs.

These competences were selected from a prior study (Warren, 1976) in which a large number of statements about student
performance had been collected from faculty members and then
organized into general clusters.

Questions to measure these four competences were written in
four academic areas—science and mathematics, humanities, social
sciences, and history and political science. All questions require the
student to make a written response. Typically about five or not more
than ten minutes are sufficient for reading the question and writing
a response to it. As many as sixty different questions were tried out
with small groups of students at several different colleges. Some of
these questions were subsequently discarded because they were too
difficult or too easy or because the responses could not be classified
reliably by faculty readers. Warren's report on the project to date
describes forty-seven questions and the major categories in which
responses are classified. One question, related to competence in
analytic thinking, is described as follows (Appendix B, p. 4):

> An exchange from Plato's *Symposium* is presented in
> which Diotima asserts that neither the wise nor the foolish

seek wisdom because the wise have it and the foolish are
ignorant of it, and Socrates asks who then seeks wisdom. The
students are to describe the dilemma involved in Socrates'
question and state the essential element of an answer. [Stu-
dents' responses are then classified into one of the following
categories:]

1. The response states the dilemma as the knowledge that
   people seek wisdom despite Diotima's assertion, and its
   resolution in the fact that the wise and foolish represent
   extremes between which many seekers after wisdom can be
   accommodated.
2. The problem is described as one of the definition of wise
   and foolish.
3. The response questions one or both of the premises that
   either the wise or the foolish don't seek wisdom.
4. The response states the student's own views about wisdom.
5. The response merely restates the question.

This line of testing is still in the development stage. Both the
ACT and ETS projects require faculty members or other trained
individuals to classify or rate the merit of students' responses and
consequently neither is well suited to mass testing. But both are
efforts to depart from the common multiple-choice test format and
both attempt to measure basic competences rather than more
specific subject-matter knowledge.

Fifty Years of Achievement Testing: Past and Future

Comprehensive achievement tests, measuring students' information across broad fields of knowledge commonly included in
college curricula, have existed for more than fifty years and have
been rather widely used. They show that during the college years
students learn a lot. Sophomores know more than freshmen. Seniors
know more than sophomores. What they know is related to what
they study and how much they have studied it. They know more
about subjects that are closely related to their major field than
about subjects less closely related to it. Nevertheless, their knowledge
tends to increase from freshmen to senior year in all subjects, except

highly specialized ones such as mathematics or foreign languages when little or no work has been done beyond the freshman or sophomore year. Surely none of this is surprising. It would be surprising if it were not so. This upward progression in the acquisition of knowledge is the mainline conclusion against which studies of special groups or more limited populations must be seen. Moreover, from some of these achievement test studies we know that comparisons of groups of students at different levels (cross-sectional studies) produce conclusions similar to those from comparisons of the same group at two points in time (longitudinal studies). This does not mean that longitudinal studies are not needed; it simply says that basically true conclusions about student achievement are not dependent on longitudinal studies.

Comprehensive achievement tests, exemplified especially by ones associated with the Graduate Record Examinations and the Educational Testing Service, are good measuring instruments. They are reliable, discriminating, and relevant to much of the undergraduate curriculum. Although they have been developed for and primarily used with students at a particular level of educational development—sophomores, for example, or seniors—they can and should be used more than they now are to test students at different levels and the same students at different times.

In the elementary and secondary schools, testing in the basic skills of reading and arithmetic has been common for many years. In recent years there has been heightened interest in the results of such testing, owing perhaps to public and legislative concerns about apparent declines in how well pupils are learning the three Rs and to tales of high school graduates who cannot read beyond the eighth-grade level. Periodic achievement testing programs are mandated in many states, and pupil progress is systematically monitored. Why is this not also occurring in higher education? There is surely some concern among taxpayers and others who finance higher education about what students are learning, a concern often expressed as a demand for greater accountability on the part of colleges and universities. Despite this concern, however, achievement tests are seldom used at any college to measure students' gains in knowledge, either longitudinally or cross-sectionally. None of the testing agencies had data of this kind of a national scope from testing programs in the 1970s.

There are both economic and educational reasons for this curious state of affairs. The economic ones are probably more influential but not necessarily more important. Someone has to pay for the tests. When tests are used for gaining admission to college or to graduate school or professional school or for obtaining college credit for knowledge a person has acquired outside college, the student obviously benefits, and thus the student can be expected to pay for taking the test. The cost to the individual is low and the benefit to the individual is high—being accepted for admission or receiving credits. When, however, achievement tests are simply used to document that seniors know a lot more than freshmen, or that students in College A make higher scores than students in College B, and when performance at some defined level is not a requirement for retention or graduation, then one cannot expect the students to pay for the tests. The Pennsylvania students did not pay to take all those tests— the Carnegie Foundation for the Advancement of Teaching paid for them. When the testing agencies need to get data from an appropriate national sample of students to establish norms on a new test, they pay for it and later recover their developmental costs from fees paid by the thousands of students who subsequently take the test for some personal purpose. If achievement tests are to be used for before-and-after measurement of students' knowledge and learning, someone other than the student must pay for it—the federal or state government, private foundations, or the colleges and universities themselves. If the colleges and universities pay, it requires putting an item in their budgets—to buy the materials, get the results scored and reported, and provide the manpower for their administration and analysis. Can they afford it? That is the economic question. Is it worth it? That is the educational question.

Obviously the public schools think that achievement testing is worth it, and the taxpayers pay for it. In the Los Angeles city schools the total cost for achievement testing is probably more than one million dollars a year. And that does not count the time involved in administering the tests or interpreting the results. Some of this testing is mandated and paid for by the State Department of Education. Some of it—tests on basic skills and common school subjects— is budgeted within the district. But in higher education there is no clear counterpart to basic skills and common subjects. As one moves up the educational ladder from elementary school to college and university, the curriculum becomes more diverse and specialized. Some common course requirements may exist at a particular college, but there are no requirements common to all colleges. Although typically some distribution requirements must be met, these can be satisfied in many different ways. For the most part, what is taught, what is emphasized in the teaching of it, and what students are expected to read are all determined by the individual faculty member. There are, of course, broad categories of subject matter which nearly all students encounter even though the specific courses may differ from one place to another. Because of all these variations, the test makers have tried to devise measures that are reasonably fair to most students and suitably applicable to most colleges; but the consequence of doing this is that the tests are less suitable for measuring student learning in specific courses or curricula. In tests of general education intended for nationwide use, the test content cannot be matched with any curriculum content, for the simple reason that there is no nationally common content or definition of general education. Nevertheless, the major tests of general education—such as the Graduate Record Area exams in science, social science, and humanities, the CLEP General exams in English composition, humanities, mathematics, natural sciences, and social sciences–history, and the UAP Area exams in humanities, natural science, and social science—do measure intellectual skills and understandings that are widely recognized as important and that are broadly relevant to undergraduate education.

ETS's Undergraduate Assessment Program is designed for use by colleges that wish to measure their students' achievement in the broad areas of general education and in specific major fields of study. It is not a program for admissions or for granting credit. Its widest use has been with college seniors. Results from having given the Area tests to freshmen, sophomores, and juniors are relatively sparse and, because of the different samples involved, do not constitute a proper base for inferring gains that might occur as one advances from freshman to senior year. No data have been published showing the scores of the same students as they progress through college. The tests can be purchased by the colleges and universities, and ETS provides a scoring and reporting service, which, as of 1978, cost $5.50 per person tested for the booklet that includes the three Area Tests, or $4.50 per person tested if the institution does its own scoring.

If the University of California wished to administer these UAP Area Tests to all undergraduates on the eight campuses, the cost to the university would be approximately half a million dollars. If they wished to give the tests to all entering freshmen and again to those same students at the end of the senior year, the cost would be about $175,000, exclusive of the manpower costs of handling the test administrations. Such a testing program deals only with the general education aspects of college study. The students' field of specialization accounts for as much time in the total program as their general education. Of the twenty-five available UAP major field tests, twenty would be appropriate for the University of California; and one might guess that these would account for about two thirds of the upper-division students. If the appropriate major field test were given to juniors at the beginning of their upper-division work and again at the end of their senior year, the cost to the university would be roughly $175,000. Thus, for a good census of students' gains in general education and in the major field or specialization, the university would need to spend about one third of a million dollars, again not counting the time of the personnel doing it.

Recommendation: Greater Use of Current Measures. I believe that students' gains in knowledge and understanding ought to be measured at all colleges and universities, at least periodically, and if not with all students, then at least with a good representative sample of them. A broad-based battery of achievement tests, relevant to the type of subject matter, knowledge, understanding, and skills one finds in most college programs, constructed and normed at a level of difficulty appropriate for college seniors, should be given to freshmen when they arrive on the campus and given to them again when they near the end of their senior year. The results, I am sure, would contribute to informed faculty discussions of educational matters on the local campus and to informed attitudes about college education among parents, state legislators, governors, federal officials, potential donors, taxpayers, and others whose views about higher education should be based on solid evidence. At a time when some people are questioning the value of higher education and even wondering whether students are really learning anything these days, we are not producing the evidence that could be produced, simply if not cheaply, by testing students at entrance and exit. So, one major activity on the agenda for achievement testing beyond the 1970s should surely be a much greater use of achievement measures with the same students at different stages of their progress through college. The accumulation of evidence of students' gains in knowledge and understanding, through longitudinal studies, would fill the most important gap that still exists in the large-scale use of achievement measures. Giving tests to samples of students, and at many different colleges, would probably be feasible financially and would certainly be worthwhile educationally. We have the instruments to do this, as well as the ingenuity to produce alternative and perhaps better instruments.

I have described two recent efforts to devise alternative measuring instruments. Both of these new developments, the Measurement Battery in the College Outcome Measures Project and the Academic Competencies in General Education, require faculty members to rate the adequacy of students' responses to the test materials. This time-consuming activity may severely limit the extent to which either of these new measures is used. Nevertheless each of the new measures reflects the beliefs of some faculty members that what is being measured is important. The content of any achievement test reflects a value. An achievement test is a criterion against which student learning is judged. Given the diversity of institutions, curricula, and students in higher education no single criterion will be adequate or applicable to all cases. For a diversity of people and programs one needs a diversity of criteria.

Recommendation: More and Different Measures. Beyond the fuller use of measures we already have, the other major development in achievement testing beyond the 1970s should be the construction of more new measures. My own thoughts about new directions in the measurement of student achievement run along three lines. The first has to do with a different way of thinking about general education. The second concerns the organization of test content around a set of major ideas and values. And the third relates to the development of a measure that seeks to integrate knowledge, attitude, and action within the individual and with respect to major objectives of general education.

General education has characteristically been defined with reference to some common body of knowledge and understanding. This more or less common body of knowledge is exemplified by required courses and by distribution requirements assuring students' exposure to the major fields of knowledge, such as the sciences, the social sciences, and the humanities. Since the typical distribution requirements can be satisfied in many different ways, as I mentioned earlier, there is no common body of knowledge to which all or most students are exposed. The distribution requirement in science might be satisfied by taking a course in chemistry or a course in geology or a course in astronomy. The distribution requirement in the social sciences might be satisfied by taking a course in economics or in sociology or in political science or some other field. Partly for this reason, some writers about general education have more or less despaired of the possibility of developing any genuinely common body of education for undergraduate students today. Partly also for this reason, some writers have wondered whether the idea of general education itself is still valid or still translatable into the college curriculum.

It seems likely that among the sources of these views is the fact that knowledge has become increasingly specialized. Particularly in the universities, the basic unit of organization and instruction is the academic department. The university is a collection of specializations. And to a considerable extent this is also true of liberal arts colleges where instruction is organized by departments. But instead of thinking about general education as a common body of knowledge, one might think of general education today, however paradoxical it may seem, as the extent to which students become acquainted with significant concepts and theories in a variety of specializations.

One can think of concepts as ways of viewing phenomena which generate new understanding. There are many examples, current and historical, that document the importance of major concepts: the concept of evolution in the biological sciences, the concept of relativity in the physical sciences, the concept of culture and cultural relativity in anthropology, the concept of systems in the social sciences, the concept of probability, concepts related to ecology that have expanded this domain to human ecology and social ecology, psychoanalytic concepts in psychology and psychiatry, the concept of alienation in sociology, the theory of tectonic plates in geology, the theory of an expanding universe in astronomy, the theory of games in mathematics. Of course, many other concepts and theories could be identified in various academic disciplines, some of which have broader consequences than others. Some concepts may have a strong effect on scholars within a field but a weak impact on laymen. What one should look for are concepts that have significant power to specialists and also significant implications for the understanding of nonspecialists—in short, concepts that not only have had an important influence within the discipline but have altered and enlarged man's view of himself and his institutions and the physical universe.

Two recent issues of *Daedalus* (Graubard, 1977a, 1977b) were devoted to the theme of discoveries and interpretations and contemporary scholarship. In these issues one finds articles about new concepts and interpretations in the sciences (physics, astronomy, archaeology, biology, geology), in the social sciences (sociology, anthropology, economics, communications), and in history, philosophy, and the arts. One could draw upon such material in writing test items. In doing so, one should avoid using highly technical terminology. The aim is not to make a vocabulary test. If the aim is to measure concepts and ideas one thinks are important for a generally educated person to understand, one should try to express the concepts in laymen's language, in so far as possible. Another potential source of test items could be interviews with faculty members who teach basic courses in a field, asking them to indicate mistaken notions commonly held by beginning students, notions the professor hopes they will no longer have when they have completed the course or majored in the field. From these interviews one could get examples of statements about an important concept or theory which the professor regards as generally correct or as illustrating greater understanding.

In an age of specialization, perhaps the generally educated person is one who has at least some minimum awareness and under-

standing of the concepts that specialists have developed for organizing and interpreting the phenomena in their specialty. An achievement test built with these ideas in mind might have special relevance
for the universities.

My second suggestion for a new kind of achievement test is
one that would be organized around major ideas and values, rather
than around basic fields of knowledge or academic disciplines. There
are major ideas and values about which general or liberal education
is presumably concerned: the development of maturity in thinking
about such ideas as liberty, justice, equality, responsibility, work,
love, beauty, and so forth. So why not develop tests that try to find
out what and how students think about such ideas and what meaning and range of application they attach to them? What is intriguing
about an attempt to devise measures for this purpose is the fact that
the meaning one attaches to such ideas provides a revelation of
values as well as understanding. Probably the format for a measure
of this sort would at least initially be similar to what Jonathan
Warren is using for his measures of competences related to general
education (see the previous section, The 1970s). One might have
standard questions and then develop ways of classifying the responses
that students make to them. A question might be "What does freedom mean and how is it exemplified in individuals and in society?"
Students' responses might range from simplistic, arbitrary, and
limited ones to ones that reveal sophistication, relativity in meaning,
and wide-ranging application. One would hope that the responses of
seniors would exhibit greater maturity of understanding than the
responses of freshmen. These topics do not reflect the way in which
undergraduate instruction is organized, but they are nevertheless
topics of pervasive importance for civilization and human relations.
Surely education should be concerned with them and test makers
should try to measure such understandings and values.

My third suggestion for a new kind of measure is one based
on the fact that many objectives of liberal education are phrased in
a way that assumes an integration within the individual of knowledge, value, and behavior. Consider the following typical statement
of an objective: "To participate as an informed and responsible
citizen and in accord with democratic ideals." In order to meet this
objective, one would probably have to combine knowledge about

society, government, and so forth, with democratic values and participation in legitimate political processes. Perhaps one of the most useful contributions that could be made in the development of new measures would be to invent a test design for revealing this ultimate integration with respect to each of several major objectives of general education.

Suppose one had an objective concerned with knowledge, value, and action in relation to the topic of human ecology. Presumably one would first want to measure what the test taker knows about the topic—that is, the relevant knowledge from biology, chemistry, health sciences, economics, and so on. Second, one might want to measure the relative importance or emphasis this person attributes to different kinds of knowledge—to scientific knowledge, economic knowledge, or psychological knowledge, for instance. Third, one might measure the general attitudes and values he or she relates to the topic. And fourth, what personal or social actions is this person willing to endorse with respect to the topic?

Here is a possible format for such a test. It is a very tentative and exploratory effort, presented for whatever suggestive merit it may have. The test might begin as follows: "The statements below all have some relevance to human ecology—that is, to man's relation to his environment, the balance of nature, pollution, and so on. Suppose you were discussing this topic, or preparing a talk or essay on it. Which of these statements would you be able to make with reasonable confidence that they are correct? Check each such statement." There would then be a list of statements—facts, principles, relevant knowledge—from academic disciplines bearing on the understanding of human ecology. Such statements could come from chemistry, biology, geology, meteorology, forestry, agriculture, health sciences, economics, demography, and the like. For example, from health sciences knowledge a statement might be "Air pollution is associated with a number of respiratory diseases" (true); from economics a statement might be "It costs less to recover wastes where they are generated, even if they have no value, than to clear them up after they have been dispersed" (true).

Following this knowledge portion of the test would be a set of statements expressing attitudes or values about human ecology. These statements could reflect scientific values, economic values, esthetic values, philosophical values, religious values. Students would indicate whether they personally agreed or disagreed with those statements.

The next section of the test might be introduced as follows: "Now, if you really were preparing a talk or essay about human ecology intended to reflect your own understanding and values, which of all the above statements would you be most likely to use and emphasize? To each fact item you have already marked above, and to each attitude statement with which you agreed, assign a rating as follows: 1 = I would certainly use this statement and give it strong emphasis; 2 = I would probably use this statement and would give it moderate emphasis; 3 = I'm not sure whether I would use this statement; or, if I did, I would give it minor emphasis."

This format provides a measure of the test taker's knowledge about the topic—the amount of knowledge within each of several fields and the breadth of knowledge across the various fields. It also provides a measure of this person's agreement or disagreement with various underlying attitudes, values, and perspectives. Thus, the emphasis one places on knowledge and on different attitudes provides a further indication of his or her general value orientation.

The final section of the test would consist of a list of social actions to which students would respond by indicating whether they generally approved or disapproved. Examples of such social actions might be the following: "Steeply grade the cost for auto license plates according to horsepower and gas mileage—an 85-horsepower, thirty-miles-per-gallon car might cost $15; whereas a 350-horsepower, ten-miles-per-gallon vehicle might cost $150." "Require beverage distributors to use returnable, recyclable containers." Many, perhaps all, of the action statements could be made parallel to some of the knowledge statements. Thus, parallel to the statement about auto license fees could be a fact statement in the first part of the test to the effect that small cars create less air pollution than large cars.

If this suggested test design stimulates test makers to try it out or to invent other models that attempt to deal with the integration of knowledge, value, and action, my tentative description of one possible model will have served a useful purpose. To the best of my knowledge, no published tests now deal with such integrative objectives.

The future value of achievement testing in higher education can be enriched by creating new or alternative kinds of measures. Students' achievement during college is and will be judged by the measures we choose to employ. The kind of achievement or competence we choose to measure reflects our belief in what is important. Neither public nor professional judgments about students' learning in college will be well served by dependence on any single type of achievement test. It is surely desirable to use more extensively, especially in longitudinal studies, the good measures we now have; but the other half of a testing agenda beyond the 1970s should focus on the creation of new instruments that can expand our knowledge about what is learned.

II

Achievement After College: Alumni

Before the 1930s no one paid much attention to college graduates. There were class reunions, of course, and alumni associations solicited contributions to the alma mater. But higher education was primarily a private affair and did not involve a very large segment of the population.

At the turn of the century there were only about 250,000 young people in colleges and universities. While in the 1930s about one and a quarter million students attended college, they were for the most part in private institutions, their education paid for by parents and philanthropists, not by the taxpayers of the state and the federal government. Indeed, it was not until 1950 that the number of students enrolled in publicly supported institutions was equal to the number enrolled in private colleges and universities.

In the 1930s John R. Tunis, to commemorate the twenty-fifth anniversary of his 1911 Harvard graduating class, wrote a book describing the lives of his classmates entitled *Was College Worthwhile?* (Tunis, 1936). For many of them it was a turbulent history. No sooner had they established themselves in their chosen vocations than World War I broke around them. After the war many had to begin all over again. Then, when they were comfortably settled in middle age, their security was again destroyed by worldwide depression.

The depression shattered the complacency of many people. It was the depression that stimulated some of the first large-scale systematic objective inquiries into the plight of college graduates. The studies showed that a college degree was not insurance against the financial hardships of depression, but they also showed that college graduates fared far better than other segments of the population.

More recently, in the 1970s, owing to the peculiar combination of inflation and depression, the previous birthrate, and a high rate of unemployment, the focus of inquiry about college graduates has again turned to their occupational and financial status. Thus major external events have been the stimulus for some large-scale systematic studies of college alumni.

Other studies of college alumni have been stimulated more by internal concerns—that is, by the colleges themselves thinking about their curriculum, about the opinions of their former students, and about the role of their graduates as adults in civic and cultural affairs. Some inquiries of this nature were stimulated following World War II by the report of the President's Commission on Higher Education and by the concern for finding a suitable balance between general education and more specialized training.

Unlike the studies of college students, which have been greatly aided by the development and widespread use of standardized achievement tests and measures of various attitudes, values, and personal traits, the study of college alumni has proceeded without benefit of standardized measuring instruments. Each inquirer has developed his own questionnaire, often without any apparent knowledge of what previous inquirers have included in theirs. Nevertheless, over the years certain kinds of questions have occurred to most investigators, and consequently it is possible at least to some extent to note similarities and differences over time in the responses of college graduates to questions about their employment, income, occupation, interests, attitudes, and other characteristics.

In this essay about college graduates I shall give primary attention to several landmark studies. Some are landmarks because they included thousands of graduates from many different institutions. Others are noteworthy because of the breadth of their content or because they provide a further base for comparison with nationwide data.

I begin, then, with a report of two studies conducted during the years of the great depression, one by the University of Minnesota, the other by the U.S. Office of Education. The focus of both of these inquiries was on the economic status of college alumni.

The 1937 Follow-Up Study of Minnesota Graduates

Because the rhetoric and rationale behind these studies have interesting parallels to current comments about the values of higher education, I begin by quoting the opening paragraphs from the Minnesota study (Eurich and Pace, 1938, pp. 1–2):

> There is widespread belief that college graduates found their job opportunities markedly curtailed by the depression. Corporations accustomed to sending representatives to college campuses all over the country to pick promising young graduates for well paid positions sent out few such representatives during the depression years and fortunate was the college graduate who found a corporation or business firm actually seeking his services. Jobs were scarce, salaries low. Prospective young school teachers found boards of education cutting pay checks, reducing staffs, not filling vacancies.
>
> Popular opinion had measured a college education by its money value. The depression graduates were disillusioned. College administrators, too, were puzzled. Some attempted to restate the purposes of education. Laymen began to doubt that a college degree conferred any benefits.
>
> Such is the picture which many persons have drawn concerning the effect of the depression on college graduates. Is it a true picture? It may be. Frequently, however, such a picture has been pieced together from a collection of frag-

ments, from the testimony of friends, from experiences from a small number of college students, perhaps from stories. To obtain a fairer, more stable and more adequate picture of the recent college graduate, much more careful and scientific techniques of gathering information must be used.

Purdue University has made such a survey of the occupational opportunities and economic status of graduates from 1928 to 1934. A continuation of this survey included the graduates of 1935. In an introduction to these studies President Elliott of Purdue said, "The extraordinary changes in the social economy of the world which have taken place during recent years have naturally caused much serious discussion of the wisdom of the established American philosophy of stimulating an ever increasing proportion of young men and women to seek the advantages of higher education. Whether this philosophy and these advantages are sound under the new order remains to be seen." Data from 2,000 students were obtained from Purdue.

President Coffman of the University of Minnesota, realizing the value of this type of study, suggested that a similar survey of the graduates of all of the colleges of the University of Minnesota be made.

The study was made. It tabulated questionnaire responses from the graduates of the colleges of agriculture, forestry and home economics, business administration, chemistry, dentistry, education, engineering and architecture, law, medicine, mines and metallurgy, nursing, pharmacy, and science, literature and the arts. Except for medicine and dentistry, only students who received bachelor's degrees were included. The graduates with medical and dental degrees were accepted for the study because students must obtain these degrees before they can legally enter those professions. There were about 17,000 Minnesota graduates between the years 1928 and 1936. Of this group addresses were available for approximately 14,000, and questionnaires were actually deliverable to almost 12,000. A little more than 6,000 former students returned the questionnaire—a response rate of 52 percent.

The questionnaire itself was quite simple. It asked the alumni to list the dates of their employment, the name of their employer or firm, the nature of their work, and their annual income, for each year since they graduated from the university. In addition, however, it included a few questions which have been the subject of continuing inquiries in more recent years; for example: How soon after receiving your degree did you get your first position? How closely related was this first position to your field of specialization at the university? How closely related is your present position to your field of specialization at the university?

In the pre-Depression years 1928, 1929, and 1930, 80 to 90 percent of the graduates said that they had obtained a job within three months after graduation. In the depths of the Depression, particularly in 1932 and 1933, slightly less than two thirds of the Minnesota graduates said that they had obtained a job within three months after graduation. By 1935 and 1936 the proportions had risen to their pre-Depression level.

Before and after the Depression roughly two thirds to three fourths of the men and women graduates said that their first job was in the same field as their university specialization. In the depths of the Depression, however, the proportion whose first jobs were in the same field as their college specialization dropped to somewhat under 60 percent. Over the nine-year period, if one considers whether their first jobs were in the "same field" or a "related field," the percentages changed very little, ranging from about 90 percent in the pre- and post-Depression years to 80 percent in the worst Depression years. Those percentages, of course, vary tremendously in relation to the field of study at the university. In the College of Science, Literature and the Arts, for example, which most people would call the liberal arts college, the proportion of men and women graduates obtaining their first job in the same field as the college specialization was rarely more than 50 percent before, during, or after the Depression, whereas in some other colleges, such as medicine, pharmacy, and dentistry, close to 100 percent of the graduates said that their first jobs were in the same field as their college specialization. These percentages were very similar for both men and women.

Despite the fact that jobs were difficult to get, Minnesota graduates were primarily employed at the professional and managerial levels even during the Depression. The United States census of 1920 classified about 2-1/2 percent of the adult population in "occupational group I," comprising such professionals as authors, clergymen, dentists, lawyers, engineers, physicians, and teachers. Of University of Minnesota graduates, 58 percent had jobs in that occupational category. Occupational group II was typified by accountants, bankers, brokers, contractors, pharmacists, inventors, managers, musicians, and proprietors. Four and seven-tenths percent of the adult population was in that occupational category in the 1920 census, but 21 percent of the University of Minnesota graduates had positions at that level. In other words, only about 7 percent of employed adults in the United States were classified in occupational groups I and II, whereas 79 percent of the graduates of the University of Minnesota held positions at those high occupational levels. Despite this favorable employment picture, it was nevertheless true that during the Depression, particularly in 1932, many college graduates found themselves unemployed from the time of graduating, presumably in June, until the beginning of the following calendar year. Both before and after the Depression the percentages unemployed for that six-month period were typically 2, 3, and 4 percent. But in 1932 the percentage unemployed for six months rose to 10 percent of the men and 11 percent of the women.

The income of college graduates presents another interesting picture. In the 1970s we have been aware that salaries are not increasing, relative to the cost of living, for many categories of employment; but in the decade of the 1930s salaries actually decreased dramatically. For example, in the first full year after graduation in the pre-Depression year of 1929, Minnesota graduates earned on the average a little over $1,900. In contrast to this, in their first year out of school, the class of 1934 averaged only a little over $1,200. Those who graduated during the Depression years of 1931 to 1934 started out with much lower salaries and subsequently received relatively smaller increases in salaries in the years immediately following. These annual salaries even during the Depression years were of course considerably higher than the average family income in the United States at that time.

The major findings of the study of Minnesota graduates were summarized as follows in the report of that study: (1) Job opportunities, measured by how soon after getting a degree the students got their first job, were markedly limited during the Depression years

of 1932 and 1933. Only 65 percent of the men graduates in 1932
and only 52 percent of the women had found jobs three months
after obtaining their degrees. In the classes of 1928 and 1936 more
than 80 percent of both men and women were employed within
three months after graduation. (2) Job preparation, measured by
the relation of the students' first job and present job to their field of
specialization in college, was more stable than job opportunity. Even
during the Depression years of 1932 and 1933 about 60 percent of
both men and women graduates got jobs in the same field as their
college specialization, and 80 percent said that their jobs were in the
same or a related field. In 1932, less than half of the graduates of
business, chemistry, engineering, and science, literature and the arts
had found jobs in their field of specialization, but in the same year
more than three fourths of the graduates of dentistry, law, medicine,
nursing, and pharmacy obtained jobs in their field of specialization.
(3) The occupational level, determined by the U.S. census classifications, at which graduates worked varied significantly during the
Depression. In 1928, 43 percent of the graduates entered jobs classified in group I, the professional level. In 1933, only 26 percent of
the graduates found initial work at that level. In 1936, the proportion finding work in the professional group rose to 39 percent. The
proportion professionally classified in each graduating class tended
to increase with the number of years since graduation. For example,
eight years after graduation, 63 percent of the men who graduated
in 1928 were employed at the professional level. (4) The average
beginning yearly salaries or earnings of men graduates ranged from
$1,900 for the class of 1928 to $1,200 for the class of 1932. In 1936
the men who graduated one year previously were earning an average
of $1,350. Recovery in salaries was slow. For women, salaries were
uniformly lower. (5) Unemployment from the date of graduation
until the beginning of the following calendar year was the fate of
10 percent of the men and 11 percent of the women graduates in
1932. In 1928 and 1936, this number was less than 4 percent.

The USOE National Survey of College Graduates

Many of the results of this Minnesota survey were confirmed
by a nationwide study of college graduates reported by the U.S.

Office of Education (Greenleaf, 1939). That study encompassed approximately 45,000 college graduates from thirty-one different colleges and universities during the years from 1928 to 1935. The questionnaire responses from these 45,000 graduates represented a return by 48 percent of the total number of graduates from those colleges during those years.

With respect to their level of employment, these graduates fared about as well as the Minnesota graduates. The 1930 U.S. census indicated that among employed men over the age of thirty-five, 5 percent were in "professional" occupations. The survey of college graduates indicated that 63 percent of the men and 67 percent of the women were in professional occupations.

As for the relationship between first jobs and field of specialization in the university, the national study indicated that the proportion of graduates whose first employment was in "the same or closely related field" was roughly 70 percent or more for men graduates before the Depression, but dropped to 52 and 53 percent during the depths of the Depression in 1932 and 1933. For the class of 1935 the percentage had only risen to 58. The corresponding percentages for women were generally similar. Between present job and field of specialization in college the relationship remained relatively constant throughout the years of this national study. Of the men, 69 to 61 percent were currently employed in their college field; for women, the range was 61 to 53 percent.

Although a majority of both men and women graduates from the years 1928 to 1935 said that they had never been unemployed since graduating from college, it was just barely a majority who said so among the graduating classes of 1932 and 1933—51 percent of the men and 56 percent of the women. The severity of unemployment can perhaps best be illustrated by indicating what proportion of college graduates said that they had been idle for a total of more than twelve months at some time or other since graduating. That fate was true of 13 percent of the men and 16 percent of the women who graduated in 1931 and of 12 percent of the men and 17 percent of the women who graduated in 1932. Even among those who graduated in the years before the Depression, 1928 and 1929, 7 percent of the men said that they had subsequently been unemployed for twelve months or longer, and 11 percent of the women indicated a similar length of unemployment. This does not mean that they were unemployed for twelve or more months consecutively; it means rather that the total number of months during which they were unemployed was twelve or longer.

Given these figures for unemployment it is not surprising to note that a rather substantial proportion of the men who graduated in the worst Depression years said that the reason for choosing their first job was "no other work was available." That was reported by 33 percent of the men who graduated in 1931, 41 percent of those who graduated in 1932, and 39 percent of those who graduated in 1933. In contrast, only 15 percent of the men graduates of 1928 and 1929 said that the reason for choosing their first job was that no other work was available. The corresponding proportions for women were considerably smaller. Even during the worst Depression years the proportion of women indicating that they chose their first job because no other work was available did not exceed 23 percent.

The Minnesota General College Study

In the late 1930s there was another study (Pace, 1941) of former Minnesota students, this one being quite different in purpose, content, and design from the previously reported study. It is described here because it represents a different kind of landmark inquiry. It was a landmark study in several respects. First its content was primarily developed by faculty members of the General College, whose purpose was to learn a great deal about the lives of young adults—their activities and interests, their problems and needs for information, their values and attitudes—as a base for thinking about developing a more relevant curriculum for General College students. Second, the questionnaire constructed for the survey was fifty-two pages long, a length that has not been equalled in any subsequent study. Moreover, this questionnaire was filled out by nearly 70 percent of all the people who received it. Third, the sample of individuals selected for receiving the questionnaire was based on a random selection of entering students at the university. This meant the design had a built-in control or comparison group, because approximately half of that sample subsequently graduated from the university and half did not, and thus comparisons could be made between grad-

uates and nongraduates. Fourth, at several places in the questionnaire there were measures or scales, as opposed to merely an assortment of interesting items, so that the responses of the graduates and
nongraduates in the survey could be compared with those of other
populations with whom those scales or measures had been used.
These included measures of job satisfaction, economic status, cultural status, liberal-conservative attitudes, and general adjustment.
And fifth, some of the items originally included in this General College survey have subsequently been used in other and nationwide
follow-up studies.

Although I was privileged to be the director of this study, the
sample design had been developed by sociologist Raymond Sletto
and about two thirds of the content of the questionnaire had been
developed by the General College faculty before my appointment
as director.

The content of the questionnaire was organized in four areas
of life which were reflected in major divisions of the General College
curriculum: earning a living, home and family life, socio-civic
affairs, and personal life. Sixteen hundred former students were
identified for inclusion in the sample, equally divided between men
and women and between those who entered the university in 1924–
25 and those who entered in 1928–29. But owing to some unavail-
able and some incorrect addresses 1,381 young adults actually
received questionnaires in December 1937, and from this group 951
responses were obtained. Subsequently interviews were held with
more than 200 respondents who were living in Minneapolis or
St. Paul.

From the vast amount of information contained in these
questionnaire responses I have selected a few items to report here,
mainly ones that provide some basis of comparison with more recent
follow-up studies. Since many follow-up studies, both the ones already described and subsequent ones, have been concerned with the
economic and occupational status of former students, this report of
the General College study begins on that topic.

With respect to occupational level we found that 50 percent
of the male graduates and 14 percent of the male nongraduates were
employed in occupational group I (professional). An additional 27
percent of the graduates and 24 percent of the nongraduates were

employed at occupational level II (semiprofessional and managerial). By way of further contrast, a survey of all employed men in the Minneapolis–St. Paul area made in 1930 showed that only 14 percent were employed at those two levels.

Although 15 to 20 percent of the male graduates began work at the lowest occupational levels, V, VI, and VII (V, semiskilled, minor clerical, and minor business; VI, slightly skilled workers; and VII, unskilled laborers), only 5 percent were at those same levels when the survey was made in 1937. Among the nongraduates in the sample, 50 percent began their work at occupational levels V, VI, or VII; and at the time of the survey 37 percent of the younger nongraduate men (1928–29 entrants) and 20 percent of the older nongraduate men (1924–25 entrants) were still employed at those levels. (The occupational levels not referred to above were III, clerical, skilled trades, and retail business; and IV, farms.)

Although only 56 percent of the men graduates and 44 percent of the women graduates said that their present jobs were in "the same field" as their university specialization, four fifths of the graduates said their university training helped them get their first jobs and gain advancement.

With respect to income as of 1937, male graduates who had entered the university in 1924–25 had a median income of $2,383 compared with an income of $2,263 for male nongraduates. Among those who entered the university in 1928–29, male graduates were earning $1,888, whereas male nongraduates earned $1,618. Both the graduates and nongraduates had median salaries considerably above that of the median U.S. family, which was $1,025 in 1935–36.

To examine job satisfaction, we used an index developed by Robert Hoppock. We found that job satisfaction was related to occupational level, to income, and to certain characteristics of jobs, such as "ample opportunities for advancement," "work possesses prestige," and "work is in line with my abilities." The level of job satisfaction was significantly higher for male graduates than for male nongraduates. The typical job-satisfaction response among the graduates is perhaps best expressed by the following items from the index: "I like it," "I like it most of the time," "I am not eager to change my job but would do so if I could get a better one," and "I like my job better than most people like theirs."

From other parts of the questionnaire here are a few examples of participation in civic and cultural activities. Of the entire population who answered the questionnaire, more than 80 percent said that they voted in the last election, that they talked about social and political problems with their friends, and that they gave money to the community chest, Red Cross, and similar agencies. As to more active civic involvement, less than a third said they had signed a petition, and less than a fourth indicated they had campaigned on behalf of a candidate, or written a letter to a public official, or attended meetings of a political club. As to cultural activities, 70 percent said they had borrowed books from the public library, and 54 percent said they had attended a musical concert during the past year. About book reading, 54 percent of the men and 82 percent of the women said they read books frequently or fairly often, and 73 percent of the men and 83 percent of the women said they read magazines frequently or fairly often.

In the study as a whole the differences between graduates and nongraduates with respect to a variety of civic, political, and cultural interests were quite small. In fact, the main differences between those who graduated and those who did not concerned the occupational level of their employment, their income, and their job satisfaction.

In the next decade, following World War II, there were two landmark studies of college graduates. One was a nationwide survey conducted by the research division of *Time* magazine. The other was a survey of graduates of Syracuse University. I designed and directed the Syracuse study; and *Time*'s survey questionnaire used some of the items I had developed for the Syracuse study. The two studies were conducted at approximately the same time, namely in 1947 and 1948.

The *Time* Survey

More than three fourths of the subscribers to *Time* magazine at that time were college graduates, and no doubt this fact accounts, at least to some extent, for *Time*'s interest in the characteristics of its clientele. The *Time* study was of a national sample of all living college graduates (Havemann and West, 1952). There were about

1,200 degree-granting colleges and universities in the late 1940s. More than 1,000 of these institutions provided a list of the names and addresses of all of their graduates whose last names began with the letters "Fa." Approximately 17,000 names and addresses were obtained. The thirteen-page questionnaire that was mailed to this list in October 1947 was returned by a little more than 9,000 of them, which represented 53 percent of the total sample and 59 percent of the net sample exclusive of bad addresses. The raw data from the *Time* survey were turned over to sociologist Robert Merton of Columbia University and the Bureau of Applied Social Research and were then analyzed in detail under Merton's general guidance by Patricia Salter West. When West completed her technical report, the publishers of *Time* invited a professional writer, Ernest Havemann, to help put the results in less technical form.

Like all studies of college graduates, the *Time* survey included questions about the economic and occupational status of the alumni. It also included questions about their attitudes toward college and some of their college experiences and various questions about their involvement in civic and cultural and political affairs and related attitudes and values.

The *Time* survey showed that 50 percent of the men graduates, and 70 percent of the women who were working, were employed in professional occupations. In contrast, only 3 percent of nongraduate U.S. men were so classified by the census bureau. An additional 34 percent of the men graduates, and 12 percent of the women who were working, were employed as proprietors, managers, and executives. According to the census bureau figures, 13 percent of the nongraduate men were employed at that occupational level. In other words, 84 percent of the male graduates and 82 percent of the female graduates who were working were employed in the two highest occupational categories.

With respect to income, the median family income in the United States in the late 1940s was $2,981, whereas the median family income of college graduates in *Time*'s national sample was $5,386.

As to whether the graduates thought that going to college had helped them in their present occupation, 73 percent of the men said it helped "a lot," 25 percent said it helped "some" and 2 percent said it helped "not at all." Almost identical percentages were obtained from the replies of the women who were working. But these percentages conceal considerable variation among the graduates in different fields of study. For instance, 95 percent of the premedical and predental majors said it helped a lot, while only 62 and 63 percent of the business administration and humanities majors and 54 percent of the social science majors agreed. It is of some interest to note that no more than 4 percent of those in any field indicated that college helped "not at all" in their present occupation.

Of course not all graduates were completely satisfied with what had been their major field of undergraduate study. For the sample as a whole, 25 percent wished they had majored in some other field. Thirty percent of those who had majored in business administration wished they had majored in something else, especially engineering. Of those who majored in the social sciences, 30 percent wished they had done otherwise, the most frequently mentioned alternative being business administration. For persons from many of the major fields, however, the alternative they now wished they had chosen was one very closely related to their original choice. For example, although 24 percent of those who had majored in the sciences or mathematics wished they had majored in something else, the field they most frequently mentioned as a better choice was a different branch of science. Although 19 percent of those who majored in engineering wished they had majored in something else, the field they most frequently mentioned as an alternative was simply a different branch of engineering.

The high value which these alumni gave to their college experience is well illustrated by the fact that when they were asked whether they would go back to college if they could do it all over again, 98 percent said they would. Moreover, 84 percent of the total group said they would go back to the same college where they had received their degrees.

I turn next to some of the results bearing on civic and political activities and on certain attitudes and opinions related to civic and governmental affairs. With respect to political activity, 79 percent of these college graduates said they had voted in their last primary or local election. Thirty percent of them indicated they had signed a petition for or against some legislation, and 23 percent stated that they had written a letter or sent a telegram to a public official during the past year. In civic affairs, 87 percent said that during the past year they had given money to the community fund or chest, 48 percent said they had attended meetings of some local civic group, 35 percent had served on a volunteer committee for some community service, 30 percent said they had some contact with a local official about a local civic problem, and 27 percent said they had collected money or carried a petition for some local civic cause.

In their attitudes about government and international affairs and civil rights, the opinions of this national sample of college graduates were characterized by the writers of the *Time* survey as predominantly anti-New Deal, as predominantly internationalist as opposed to isolationist, and as sharply divided (tolerant versus prejudiced) about civil rights. Anti-New Deal attitudes were strongest among the older alumni. They were quite firm in the view that "democracy depends fundamentally on the existence of free business enterprise," that "the best government is the one which governs least," and that "government planning should be strictly limited, for it almost invariably results in the loss of essential liberties and freedom." The attitudes of younger alumni, while not anti-New Deal, were not pro-New Deal either—their responses being more or less equally divided pro and con. With respect to international affairs, most alumni were favorable toward the role and authority of the United Nations; and they disagreed with the notions that allowing more immigrants to this country would lower the standard of culture and that lowering our tariffs to permit more foreign goods would lower our standard of living. Moreover they did not feel that ideological differences between countries were irreconcilable. Internationalist sentiments were more prevalent among the younger graduates. With respect to civil rights the responses of a majority of alumni were quite clearly on the side of tolerance: for example, 80 percent or more of them agreed that "all Americans should have equal opportunity in social, economic, and political affairs" and disagreed with the statement that "children of minority groups or other races should play among themselves." Further, two thirds of them disagreed with the statement that "foreigners usually have peculiar and annoying habits"; and more than half of them disagreed with the statement that "agitators and troublemakers are more likely to be foreign-born citizens than native Americans." The authors of the *Time* report classified as tolerant only those who responded on the tolerant side to all four of the above statements, and they classified as prejudiced those whose responses were on the prejudiced side in at least two of the four statements. On that basis 38 percent were described as tolerant and 32 percent as prejudiced. The extent of prejudice was considerably less among the younger alumni than among those who were fifty years of age or over.

The Study of Syracuse Alumni

The importance of the Syracuse study lies in the scope of its content, the structure of the questionnaire itself, and the rationale and purpose behind this content and structure. Because the Syracuse survey reflected an emergent set of ideas about the design and purpose of an alumni questionnaire, a brief account of the origin of those ideas is in order.

My prior experience with the General College's study of former Minnesota students, and especially the experience of trying to make sense out of and usefully capitalize on the responses to more than 1,000 separate questionnaire items, led me to believe that future alumni surveys should be built around a set of well-defined scales or measures that would enable one to report scores rather than responses to a whole array of separate items. If one considers the purpose of an alumni survey to be an evaluation of the undergraduate college experience, and if one thinks of alumni as the products of that experience, then an alumni survey might be viewed as a battery of achievement or attainment measures. Just as batteries of achievement tests measuring students' knowledge in sciences, social sciences, humanities, and fine arts are relevant to evaluating students' development and educational programs while they are still students, a comparable battery of measures for alumni would deal with information, attitudes, and behavior relevant to the position of people after they leave college. How might such measures be constructed?

Guttman Scales. During World War II while I was working in the Navy Department, my friend and colleague Louis Guttman in the Pentagon was developing a radically new theory of psycholog-

ical measurement. Classical test theory was based on an analysis of
responses, on developing measures to discriminate reliably between
the responses of individuals. Guttman's concept was based on an
analysis of content, of finding a universe of content which would be
unidimensional in the sense that the items belonging to it would
form a coherent hierarchy. Given such a universe of content, the responses of individuals to any set of items within it would form a
scale which had perfect reliability and exact meaning. If the scale
consisted of seven items and you knew that an individual got a score
of four, you would also know exactly which four of the seven items
had been answered. The beauty of this theory in practice is that a
relatively few items can produce a very reliable and meaningful
measure. Guttman successfully developed many such scales, measuring morale, attitude toward officers, post-war educational plans, and
so on. I developed some similar kinds of scales for use in the Navy.

American University Alumni Survey. After the war, during
the six months between my departure from the Navy Department
and my arrival as a faculty member at Syracuse University, I had an
opportunity to design an alumni survey for American University in
Washington, D.C. For one major part of the alumni questionnaire I
tried to develop Guttman-type scales. These were checklists of activities related to the broad fields of social science, humanities and arts,
and science. To what extent do alumni participate in political affairs,
civic affairs, religion, art, music, literature, and science? The instructions were simply to "check each activity which you have engaged in
during the past year." There were ten activities in each scale, and in
each of them the items followed a roughly similar pattern: a grad-
ual ascension from commonplace and easy-to-do things to more
sophisticated activities which would imply a deeper level of interest
and commitment; the scale was designed so that participation in the
more complex or uncommon activities tended to subsume participation in all the simpler and commoner ones.

In the scale of activities related to art, for example, the first
item merely inquired whether this was a topic of conversation with
the respondents' friends. Beyond that, have they visited a gallery or
museum? More specifically, have they been to any exhibition of
contemporary painting? Have they read any books or attended any
lectures about art? Have they bought a painting or other art work

for themselves? Do they do anything in particular to support art with their money or their services in the community? Do they attempt anything creative themselves?

In analyzing the responses of alumni to each of these ten-item activity checklists, I found that usually seven, eight, or nine of the items did indeed form a scale pattern of the kind described by Louis Guttman. There were usually one or two items which seemed not to belong to that particular universe of content. It was obvious, however, that scales of this kind could be constructed successfully for measuring the outcomes of general or liberal education as reflected in the behavior and interests of former students.

The second major part of the alumni questionnaire consisted of nine groups of items measuring opinions. These opinion measures dealt with the topics of art, music, literature, religion, politics, civic affairs, science, government, and international relations. The opinion scales, in other words, covered the same general territory that had been covered by the various activity scales. The unique aspect of these opinion scales was that I tried to write statements which might be regarded as generalizations of concepts that were widely accepted by experts in the particular field, although the statements themselves were expressed as opinions and indeed could easily be regarded as opinions by most people. For example, among the opinions related to art was the following statement: "What is good and bad in art is a matter of personal taste." Experts in the field of art disagree with this statement. They believe there are esthetic criteria which transcend mere personal taste. Here is another example, this time from the opinion items about politics: "Sending letters and telegrams to congressmen is a waste of time, for it has little influence on legislation." Experts in the field of politics and particularly those who have closely observed the legislative process and the activities of legislators disagree with that statement. From their experience they say that congressmen do pay attention to their mail and that it does indeed influence their action. Because the opinion statements were of this type, it was possible to assign a score to the responses of alumni indicating how often their opinions coincided with the opinions of experts.

A special analysis of these activity and opinion scales was made for the research division of *Time* magazine when they were developing the questionnaire for their proposed nationwide survey. Subsequently the *Time* research staff decided to use the two activities scales related to politics and civic affairs and the four opinion scales dealing with politics, government, civic affairs, and international relations. They did not use the scales related to the arts and humanities and science. In many respects the alumni study at American University was a pretest for the much larger study made the following year at Syracuse University. The results of the study at American University were never published. They exist only in a typewritten report prepared for the president of the university.

Elements in the Syracuse Survey. At Syracuse University, beginning in the summer of 1947 and continuing for two years, the faculty and administration engaged in a wide-ranging self-survey of the current status of the institution, leading to recommendations for its growth and development in the postwar years. The survey dealt with such matters as administration, finance, library, buildings and grounds, undergraduate curriculum, research activities, graduate programs, and many other matters. The self-survey committee dealing with undergraduate curriculum was concerned mainly with general education. In pursuing that concern, they gave various achievement tests to sophomores and to seniors, and many discussions were devoted to the objectives of general education. The possible value of a survey of Syracuse graduates was presented to the committee, which then approved the undertaking. At this point the various activity and opinion scales devised for American University were somewhat expanded and improved for use in the Syracuse study.

Beyond the activity scales and the measures of opinion, the Syracuse survey included a third major element: a list of objectives or goals of higher education. For each statement in the list, alumni were asked, "How much did your college experience help you in this knowledge, skill, or understanding?" They could respond by checking "much," "some," "little or nothing." The report of President Truman's Commission on Higher Education, which had recently been published, contained an extensive discussion of the goals of higher education. And so in developing the items for the Syracuse questionnaire, I simply wrote very abbreviated versions of those goals. The idea of asking former students to rate the extent to which their college experience helped them in attaining various goals is surely an obvious one, but to the best of my knowledge it had not been done in any previous major alumni survey. The basic structure of the Syracuse questionnaire, then, consisted of three sets of measures: 1) measures of the extent of alumni's involvement in various civic and cultural affairs; 2) measures of the extent to which alumni's concepts and values were similar to those of experts in the relevant fields; and 3) alumni's ratings of the extent to which the college experience helped in the attainment of various goals.

The sample of alumni included all for whom mailing addresses were available in the graduating classes of 1947, '42, '37, '32, '27, '17, and '07. Half of the questionnaires, or 2,500, were returned. The questionnaires were mailed in March 1948. The management of the survey, and the analysis and interpretation of its results, was carried out by Donald G. Wallace for his doctoral dissertation (Wallace, 1949). Although portions of the results have been reported in journal articles and chapters in books and in a local report to the Syracuse University faculty, the complete data from the study are found only in Wallace's dissertation. Some of the results reported here have not been previously reported in generally available sources. These results are based on approximately 2,000 Syracuse alumni; they do not include the graduates before 1927.

Like other alumni surveys, the Syracuse inquiry included questions about the economic and occupational status of the graduates. It revealed that the median family income of Syracuse graduates as of 1948 was $5,316, which may be compared with the median family income in 1946 of $2,981, as reported by the census bureau. With respect to occupational level, the proportion of Syracuse graduates employed in group I, professional, was 42 percent among the men and 57 percent among the employed women. Group II, described as semiprofessional and managerial, contained 28 percent of Syracuse men and 17 percent of employed women. In other words, 70 percent of Syracuse men graduates and 74 percent of employed women graduates were at the top two occupational levels.

With respect to the relationship between their first job and their major field of study, 47 percent of the men and 63 percent of the employed women said the job was in the same field; an addi-

tional 30 percent of the men and 18 percent of the women said it
was in a related field. As to their present job, 41 percent of the men
and 39 percent of the employed women said it was in the same field
as their undergraduate major; an additional 34 percent of the men
and 23 percent of the women said it was in a related field. Relatively
few of the graduates, however, had any regrets about their choice of
a major field: one fifth said they wished they had chosen another
field.

Some indication of their attitude toward their undergraduate
experience at Syracuse University is indicated by replies to the question "Would you recommend Syracuse to a close friend who is
considering going to college?" Eighty-eight percent of the men and
87 percent of the women said they would.

A more diagnostic indication of college benefits is shown in
Table 13. For each of a list of eighteen objectives the alumni indicated how much help their college experience had given them in
attaining the relevant knowledge, skill, or understanding (the percentages in the table do not add across to 100 because of occasional
omissions, usually only 2 to 4 percent). More than nine out of ten
of these college graduates believed their college experience had
helped them "much" or "some" with respect to preparing for a
vocation, critical thinking, understanding other people, and developing social competence. More than eight out of ten of them thought
their college experience had helped them much or some with respect
to effective writing and speaking, self-understanding, understanding
social, economic, and political issues, and the understanding and
enjoyment of literature. Approximately three fourths of the graduates
attributed some or much help to their college experience with respect
to objectives related to effective citizenship, the development of a
personal philosophy, and making a wise vocational choice. For this
total group of alumni, the objectives to which the college experience
made considerably less contribution were of two kinds: first, goals
that were not prominent or pervasive or explicit in the offerings of
the college, such as those related to health and to marital and family
adjustment; and second, goals that had a fairly specific or restricted
location in the curriculum, such as understanding science and technology and developing an understanding and enjoyment of art and
music.

Table 13. Ratings of Progress Toward Objectives: Syracuse Alumni Study

Objectives	How much did your college experience help you in this knowledge, skill or understanding?		
	Much	Some	Little or Nothing
1. Developing good health habits.	12	42	43
2. Understanding the bases of personal and community health.	13	46	37
3. Writing clearly and effectively.	39	45	13
4. Speaking easily and well.	34	47	17
5. Developing social competence.	48	41	7
6. Understanding other people.	55	36	6
7. Preparing for a satisfactory family and marital adjustment.	12	37	47
8. Discovering personal strengths and weaknesses, abilities and limitations.	38	47	13
9. Understanding world issues and pressing social, political and economic problems.	31	48	18
10. How to participate effectively as a citizen.	22	52	23
11. Understanding scientific developments and processes and their applications in society.	24	40	32
12. How to think clearly, meet a problem and follow it to a right conclusion without guidance.	47	43	7
13. Developing an understanding and enjoyment of literature.	32	45	20
14. Developing an understanding and enjoyment of art and music.	23	35	38
15. Understanding the meaning and values in life.	27	52	18
16. Developing a personal philosophy and applying it in daily life.	26	47	23
17. Making a wise vocational choice.	30	39	27
18. Preparing for a vocation.	57	32	9

One of the main emphases in the analysis of the Syracuse alumni survey was on examining their attainments in light of their major fields as students. These examinations show clearly that adult attainment is strongly related to the undergraduate major. For example, although 32 percent of the total sample indicated they received "much" help with respect to developing an understanding and enjoyment of literature, 66 percent of the men and 82 percent of the women who had majored in the humanities in the college of liberal arts gave this response. Similarly, although only 23 percent of the total group gained "much" help with respect to developing an understanding and enjoyment of art and music, 77 percent of the men and 92 percent of the women whose undergraduate work was in the college of fine arts gave a "much" response to this item. A similar sharp differentiation occurs with respect to the objective of understanding science and technology. While only 24 percent of the total group said college had given them much help in that regard, among men who were in the college of applied science or in the college of forestry or who were science majors in the college of liberal arts, and among women who were science majors in the college of liberal arts, roughly two thirds thought they received much help from college in understanding science and technology. In the social science field, 63 percent of the men and 50 percent of the women who were social science majors in the college of liberal arts gained much help from their college experience in understanding social, political, and economic issues, compared with 31 percent for the total group of alumni. With respect to effective writing, an objective strongly emphasized in the humanities, one finds that 64 percent of the men and 60 percent of the women who were humanities majors in the college of liberal arts said they got much help in becoming effective writers, compared with 39 percent for the total group of alumni. And finally, the highest percentages of "much" responses with respect to vocational preparation were found among the men graduates from the most vocationally oriented programs, such as the college of forestry, the college of applied science, and the college of fine arts, and the women graduates from the college of fine arts and the school of business. Typically around 70–75 percent of these various groups received much benefit, compared with 57 percent for the total group of alumni.

There is of course a good deal of common sense reflected in these different ratings of college benefits. One would surely expect that science students would be most likely to attain science goals, social science students to attain social science goals, and so on. These results are similar to the achievement test results I reported in the previous chapter, which showed that the highest scores on different parts of the tests were made by students whose major field or area of interest was most clearly related to that part of the test.

What I have just reported are self-estimates of educational benefits, personal estimates made by alumni as they look back on their college experience. What I report next are more objective indicators—namely the activities in which alumni are currently engaged and the extent to which their current opinions about various matters are congruent with the opinions of experts in those matters. These more objective results are shown in the next four tables.

The first set of results, Table 14, shows the pattern of activities of Syracuse men graduates from different major fields. Note, for example, that the current involvement in science-related activities of alumni whose undergraduate programs were most clearly related to the sciences—those in applied science, forestry, and liberal-arts science—was significantly above the average for all men in the sample. Then note that for science majors in the college of liberal arts, there were no activity scales on which their mean score was significantly below the average of all men, whereas for the graduates of the college of applied science, four of the seven activity scales were significantly below the university mean, and among those who graduated from the college of forestry, one of the seven scales was significantly below the all-university mean. Note next the differences between those who had graduated from the school of business and those who had majored in the social sciences within the college of liberal arts. The business graduates were not significantly above the mean with respect to any of the activity scales, and they were significantly below the mean on four of them. The graduates in social sciences within the college of liberal arts were above the mean on five of the seven scales, significantly so on two of them, and were significantly below the mean on only one scale.

The next table, Table 15, reports similar results on the activity scales for the women graduates. Here the scores of each major curriculum group are compared with the total score of all women in the sample. The pattern of results for the women graduates is generally similar to that of the men, although the differences between the various groups of women are in some cases not as sharp, perhaps because women have been less strongly oriented than men toward specialized or vocational goals.

Tables 16 and 17 report the results on the various opinion measures. These brief opinion measures were intended to be indicators of knowledge in the sense that the score reflects the extent to

Table 14. Pattern of Activities of Syracuse Men Graduates from Different Major Fields

	Applied Science	Business	Fine Arts	Forestry	Liberal Arts-Sciences	Liberal Arts-Social Sciences	Liberal Arts-Humanities
++	Science		Art Music Literature	Science	Science	Politics Literature	Literature Music
+		Religion	Religion Politics Civic affairs	Civic affairs	Music	Civic affairs Music Art	Art Religion Civic affairs Politics
−	Religion Civic affairs	Civic affairs Politics	Science	Religion Politics Music Art	Literature Religion Art Politics Civic affairs	Religion	Science
−−	Politics Literature Music Art	Literature Music Art Science		Literature		Science	

++ = activity scores significantly above the mean of all men.
+ = activity scores above the mean, but not significantly.
− = activity scores below the mean, but not significantly.
−− = activity scores significantly below the mean of all men.

Table 15. Pattern of Activities of Syracuse Women Graduates from Different Major Fields

	Business	Fine Arts	Home Economics	Liberal Arts-Sciences	Liberal Arts-Social Sciences	Liberal Arts-Humanities
++		Art Music		Science Religion		Literature
+			Religion Science	Music Politics Civic affairs	Politics Literature	Politics Civic affairs Music
−	Religion Civic affairs Literature Politics	Civic affairs Religion Literature Science Politics	Civic affairs Politics Art		Civic affairs Religion Science Music	Religion Science Art
− −	Science Music Art		Literature Music	Art	Art	

+ + = Activities score significantly above the mean of all women.
+ = Activities score above the mean, but not significantly.
− = Activities score below the mean, but not significantly.
− − = Activities score significantly below the mean of all women.

Table 16. Opinions of Syracuse Men Graduates from Different Major Fields Compared to Experts' Opinions

	Applied Science	Business	Fine Arts	Forestry	Liberal Arts-Sciences	Liberal Arts-Social Sciences	Liberal Arts-Humanities
++			Art Music Literature		Science Music Civic relations	Government Civic relations Politics Literature World Science	Literature Art Music Government
+	Politics	Philosophy		Philosophy	Literature Art Philosophy Government	Music Art	Civic relations World Science Politics Philosophy
−	World Philosophy Music Literature Art Science Civic relations Government	Politics World Science	World Philosophy Civic relations Politics Government Science	Science Politics World Literature	Politics World	Philosophy	
− −		Civic relations Music Government Art Literature		Civic relations Government Music Art			

+ + = Opinion score significantly above the mean of all men (representing high agreement with experts).

+ = Opinion score above the mean, but not significantly.

− = Opinion score below the mean, but not significantly.

− − = Opinion score significantly below the mean of all men.

Table 17. Opinions of Syracuse Women Graduates from Different Major Fields

	Business	Fine Arts	Home Economics	Liberal Arts-Sciences	Liberal Arts-Social Sciences	Liberal Arts-Humanities
+ +		Art Music			Government Civic relations World	Literature Philosophy
+	Science		Politics Art Civic relations Philosophy Science Music	Science Politics Philosophy World	Politics Literature Science	World Music Government
−	Philosophy World Government Politics Civic relations	Literature Philosophy Civic relations Politics Science	World Government	Government Literature Civic relations Art Music	Music Art Philosophy	Art Civic relations Politics Science
− −	Literature Art Music	World Government	Literature			

+ + = Opinion score significantly above the mean of all women (representing high agreement with experts).
+ = Opinion score above the mean, but not significantly.
− = Opinion score below the mean, but not significantly.
− − = Opinion score significantly below the mean of all women.

which concepts and generalizations held by the alumni agree with
the concepts and generalizations held by faculty experts in the various fields. In the results for men, the differences between liberal arts
majors and those whose programs were in one of the professional
schools are particularly striking, as are comparisons between social
science majors and graduates from the school of business. The results
for women reveal a similar pattern of differences between the liberal
arts and the more professionally oriented programs, as well as between the graduates in fine arts and those who had majored in the
humanities. In general, the women's scores fall in the middle two
categories more than the men's do.

All of the foregoing comparisons between graduates from
different fields produce a basically similar pattern of results. Whether
one looks at the alumni's own opinions about how helpful their university experience had been in various respects, or whether one
examines their current activities as young to middle-aged adults in
their respective communities, or whether one examines the extent to
which their generalizations and concepts about various topics are
similar to those of faculty experts in their respective fields, the conclusion is the same: the pattern of activities and interests, of concepts,
and of retrospective opinions of these former university students cor-
responds neatly and clearly to what had been the pattern or major
emphasis of their experience when they were students.

The Calvert Survey of Men Graduates in Liberal Arts

Following the *Time* survey, the next alumni study of national
scope was made in 1963. The study was done at the Survey Research
Center of the University of California, Berkeley, under the direction
of Robert Calvert, Jr. (1969). Inspired in part by the *Time* survey,
Calvert's study, like the one at Syracuse, was concerned with much
more than the occupational and economic status of former students.
It delved into their attitudes about their own education and its
benefits, and also their involvement in a variety of civic and cultural
activities. The particular importance of this study lies not so much
in its scope as in the fact that it was concentrated on the lives of men
who had graduated with a major in one of the traditional liberal
arts fields: the sciences, the social sciences, the humanities, literature,
and the arts. Men whose undergraduate work had been primarily in

some vocational or technical program such as engineering or business were not included in the survey. It is particularly interesting today, given the skepticism which many people have about the value of majoring in the liberal arts, to review the subsequent fate of a large number of men, all of whom were liberal arts graduates.

One hundred colleges and universities participated in this survey. They included liberal arts colleges of moderate size and universities both public and private. The sample consisted of men who had graduated in 1958, 1953, and 1948. Since the survey questionnaire was mailed in 1963, these former students had completed their bachelors degrees five, ten, and fifteen years previously. Some 18,000 questionnaires were mailed; nearly 11,000 returns were received, representing 60 percent of the total or 70 percent of the questionnaires that were actually delivered. The results I have chosen to report from this survey are primarily ones that provide a basis for comparison with other alumni studies.

The first set of results listed below relates to occupation. We see, for example, that although most of the men did not select their occupational or career goal until after they graduated from college, they were nevertheless quite satisfied with their occupational status. Moreover, despite the fact that only 39 percent of them said they had chosen their occupational goal before or during college, 73 percent said they received good preparation for their vocational life.

Occupation

1. Occupational level: approximately two thirds at professional or managerial level
2. Time when occupational or career goal selected:

before or during college	39%
after graduating from college	46
no answer	15

3. Time unemployed or between jobs since graduation:

never	66%
1 to 4 months	21
5 to 11 months	7
12 months or more	3
no answer	3

4. Do you wish you were in an occupation other than your present one?

    yes   10%

5. How much do you like the kind of work you are doing?

    very much   69%

    fairly much   22

    dislike slightly or greatly   6

    no answer   3

6. To what extent does your current job give you an opportunity to use your special abilities?

    to a high degree   55%

    moderately   31

7. "I received good preparation for my vocational life":

    agree   73%

    disagree   27

8. Estimated median salary (in 1963):

    5 years after graduation $ 8,000

    10 years after graduation $10,500

    15 years after graduation $13,000

Perhaps some of the reasons they regard their liberal arts education so highly are suggested in the next set of responses from the survey—responses related to the general values they attribute to their liberal education.

Value of a Liberal Education

1. In meeting selected objectives, did your education:

    provide a broad fund of knowledge about different fields?   yes   80%

    develop a fund of knowledge useful in later life?   yes   80

    develop the ability to get along with different types of people?   yes   72

    develop moral capacities, ethical standards, and values?   yes   68

    train you in depth in at least one field?   yes   59

develop social poise?	yes	53%
develop a sense of responsibility for participating in community and civic affairs	yes	53

(Note: about 5% to 6% gave no answer to the above items.)

give you good training in how to express your ideas clearly?	agree	69

2. General attitudes:

The courses I took were on the whole quite stimulating and interesting	agree	86%
I would advise a high school graduate to take a liberal arts major	agree	78
If you could start college all over again, would you still attend the same college you got your degree from?	yes	57
	not sure	29
	no	14

Their involvement in a variety of activities related to cultural, civic, and other matters is shown in the next set of responses. Whether the proportion of participants is judged to be relatively high, moderate, or low is of course a debatable issue. It does seem reasonably clear, however, that roughly one fourth to one third of these men engaged in community activities that were fairly time-consuming, such as working on fund-raising drives for charitable organizations or for a church, being engaged in some leadership role with respect to a youth group, and serving on a committee or board for their church.

Cultural and Other Activities in Past Twelve Months

1. Cultural activities

attended one or more public lectures	68%
attended two or more theatrical productions	66
visited an art museum	60
read more than five books of fiction	43
participated in a literary or art discussion or study group	39

attended two or more opera or symphony concerts	36
read more than five nonfiction books (not related to work)	36

2. Civic activities

worked on fund-raising drives for the United Fund or other charitable organization	35%
attended two or more PTA meetings	34
led or assisted in the leadership of a scout troop or other youth group	25
belonged to a service club	20

3. Religious activities

attended religious services fairly regularly	58%
worked on fund raising for a church	30
served on a church board or committee	26

4. Political activities

wrote or talked to a public official about a current program or proposed bill	45%
belonged to a political club or political action group	18

5. Activities related to alma mater

attended a college alumni function or visited the campus	50%
gave money to the college or university	48

Aside from the impact of a liberal arts education on male graduates' professional lives, it is evident that interests in the fine arts and in civic, religious, and political affairs—often regarded as evidence of liberal arts values—continue to be expressed in these graduates' lives.

The NORC Alumni Survey

There were two more alumni surveys of nationwide scope conducted during the 1960s. The first was a survey of relatively recent graduates made in 1969 by the National Opinion Research Center (NORC). Samples of alumni from the graduating class of

1961 from 135 colleges and universities formed the base for NORC's study. The second survey was conducted at UCLA and included graduates from the class of 1950 from 74 different colleges and universities across the country. The NORC study, then, reports information about people who had graduated seven years earlier, whereas the UCLA study concerned some who had graduated eighteen years before.

The results of the NORC study have been reported in a book written for the Carnegie Commission on Higher Education (Spaeth and Greeley, 1970). Partly because the results of the NORC study are readily available in this book and partly also because the content of the study, while including a wealth of information and analysis, contains relatively little that can be directly compared with other alumni surveys, my report of selected highlights from the NORC survey is relatively brief.

With respect to the occupational status of these recent graduates, 71 percent were in professional positions and an additional 19 percent were managers, proprietors, and officials. Thus 90 percent of them were employed at the two highest occupational levels. It is also of interest to note that one third of these recent graduates had subsequently attained some higher degree. Their judgment about the relationships between college and work is illustrated by their answers to the following question: "How well would you say each of the following prepared you for the job you currently hold?" With respect to their undergraduate major, 78 percent said very or moderately well; with respect to college training in general, 86 percent said very or moderately well; and with respect to graduate or professional school, for those who went, 87 percent said very or moderately well.

The alumni's judgments about the influence of their college experience on them in relation to a broader range of educational outcomes are summarized next. The alumni responded to the statement "Please rate the extent to which your college affected you in each of these ways." The percentages that gave a "greatly" or "somewhat" response were as follows:

Developed my abilities to think and express myself	87%
Gave me a broad knowledge of the arts and sciences	77

Expanded my tolerance for people and ideas   75

Helped me to learn how to make my own decisions   73

Helped me to learn how to get along with others   68

Trained me for my present job   67

Helped me formulate the values and goals of my life   64

Further indications of their attitudes toward college were provided by the following ratings. Three fourths of the alumni rated the faculty as excellent or good; 71 percent rated the caliber of classroom teaching as excellent or good; slightly more than two thirds of them rated the curriculum and course offerings as excellent or good. Somewhat in contrast, 46 percent rated personal contacts with the faculty as having been excellent or good. In their general attitudes or feelings about their undergraduate college or university, the responses showed that 86 percent had clearly favorable feelings, whereas only 4 percent had clearly unfavorable feelings.

The NORC study, like some of the previous alumni surveys, had some items in it asking the alumni to indicate how frequently they engaged in various cultural activities. Four fifths of these recent alumni said they frequently or occasionally read nonfiction; two thirds said they frequently or occasionally read fiction and listened to classical or serious music; more than half reported that they frequently or occasionally went to plays and to museums and art galleries; two fifths indicated that they frequently or occasionally went to concerts; and one fourth said they frequently or occasionally read poetry. With respect to their engagement in nearly all of these activities they also felt that college had been a great or moderate influence.

Among the many relationships, correlations, and analyses reported in the book, two in particular provide some confirmation of the results obtained in other alumni studies. The authors devised what they described as an "interest in the arts" index and also a "serious reading" index, and then compared the index levels of alumni in different career fields. For example, on the "interest in the arts" index, among those whose career field was in the humanities,

44 percent were in the highest quartile of the total alumni group. In contrast, only 11 percent of those having engineering careers, and only 14 percent of those in a business field, were in the top quarter of the total group with respect to their interest in the arts. A similar contrast was reported for the "serious reading" index. Among those who were in the humanities, 52 percent were in the top quarter of the total group of alumni, compared with only 10 percent and 11 percent, respectively, of those whose career fields were engineering and business.

The UCLA Survey

During the first few months of 1969, an eighteen-page questionnaire was sent to representative graduates of the class of 1950 from seventy-four different colleges and universities, large and small, public and private, and from all parts of the country. The questionnaire was returned by somewhat more than 8,000 of them, that number being 58 percent of those who received it. The questionnaire inquired about many of their current activities, interests, viewpoints, and beliefs, their reflections on their college education, their college experiences, and their present occupation, income, politics, religion, and other conditions about themselves and their lives.

The design of the questionnaire was generally similar to that used in the earlier Syracuse study. It consisted first of a series of activities scales measuring the nature and extent of alumni involvement in community affairs, national and state politics, art, music, drama, literature, education, religion, science, intercultural affairs, and international affairs. It also included a number of measures of the alumni's attitudes toward social trends and social issues such as government and international affairs, civil rights, censorship, and the status of women. Also, as in the Syracuse study, there was a checklist of educational objectives, and the alumni were asked to indicate the extent to which they felt their college experience had influenced them in those directions. And finally, it contained a good many questions about their particular school and college experiences and their present occupation, income, and other matters. In a sense, then, the aim of the UCLA study was to obtain, from a national population of college graduates, responses to a broad range of questions similar in content to what had previously been presented to the graduates of a single institution, namely Syracuse. In a more significant sense, the aim of the study was to make a national evaluation of the outcomes of higher education, as such outcomes can be inferred from the activities, values, and opinions of former students, and to explore the relationships among such outcomes and particular college experiences and the type of college attended.

Many of the results from this study have been reported in two books I wrote for the Carnegie Commission on Higher Education (Pace, 1972, 1974). What I shall report here are a few highlights from these books, as well as some additional information not previously reported.

With respect to the educational benefits of college going, the 8,000 alumni were asked, "In thinking back to your undergraduate experience in college or university, to what extent do you feel that you were influenced or benefited in each of the following respects?" Following are the percentages of those who responded "very much" or "quite a bit" to each of these benefits: "Vocabulary, terminology, and facts in various fields of knowledge"—79 percent; "critical thinking—logic, inference, the nature and limitations of knowledge"—72; "personal development—understanding one's abilities and limitations, interests, and standards of behavior"—66; "background and specialization for further education in some professional, scientific, or scholarly field"—64; "awareness of different philosophies, cultures, and ways of life"—64; "bases for improved social and economic status"—63; "writing and speaking—clear, correct, effective communication"—63; "broadened literary acquaintance and appreciation"—62; "social development—experience and skill in relating to other people"—61; "appreciation for individuality and independence of thought and action"—61; "tolerance and understanding of other people and their values"—56; "science and technology—understanding and appreciation"—54; "development of friendships and loyalties of lasting value"—53; "aesthetic sensitivity —appreciation and enjoyment of art, music, drama"—45; "vocational training—skills and techniques directly applicable to a job"— 43; "citizenship—understanding and interest in the style and quality of civic and political life"—37; and "appreciation of religion—moral and ethical standards"—31.

One needs to remember that these percentages are composites from people who had attended very different types of institutions. For example, with respect to vocational training, although the composite percentage was 43 percent, among those who had attended institutions with a strong vocational emphasis, such as the colleges of engineering and sciences, the colleges that have a strong emphasis on teacher training, and colleges that have a variety of vocational curricula, such as the state colleges, the percentages were much higher, namely from 53 to 61 percent; and from alumni of the institutions having the least emphasis on vocational training, namely the liberal arts colleges, the corresponding figures were only approximately 25 to 33 percent. Similarly, only 54 percent of the total group of alumni received very much or quite a bit of benefit with respect to understanding science and technology, compared to 94 percent of the graduates from the colleges of engineering and science.

When one looks at objectives that are primarily related to the humanities, namely the awareness of different philosophies, cultures, and ways of life, broadened literary acquaintance, and appreciation and enjoyment of art, music, and drama, it is the graduates of the liberal arts colleges who are most likely to have been benefited in those respects, and graduates from the colleges of engineering and science who are least likely. When one looks at objectives related to personal and interpersonal development, such as friendships, tolerance, appreciation of individuality, and social development, the highest percentages of "very much" or "quite a bit" responses came from alumni of the institutions having the highest proportions of full-time resident students. These tend to be the relatively small liberal arts colleges, as contrasted with the large and often urban state universities and state colleges, many of which have much smaller proportions of resident students. For the objective related to religion and moral and ethical standards, it is the graduates from the strongly denominational liberal arts colleges, both Protestant and Catholic, who were most likely to say they received very much or quite a bit of benefit in attaining that objective, namely 74 percent, compared with 31 percent for the nationwide alumni sample. There is, in other words, a broad pattern of relationship between the nature of the college experience and the type of institution attended, on the one hand, and the attainment of objectives congruent with those differences in the college experience and environment, on the other.

A similar pattern of relationships is found when one looks at the current activities of these former students. For example, in activities related broadly to the humanities, especially art, literature, and drama, it is the graduates from the liberal arts colleges who are most fully engaged in such matters. It is also the graduates of the most selective liberal arts colleges who are most actively engaged in activities related to intercultural affairs. In contrast, with respect to all four of these areas of activity, it is the graduates from the colleges of engineering and science and from the state colleges and regional universities who are least involved. Also as one would expect, graduates of the strongly denominational colleges are most actively engaged in matters related to religion, graduates from the colleges of engineering and science are most actively engaged in matters related to science, and graduates from colleges emphasizing teacher training are most actively engaged in matters related to education. In short, the reported behavior is consistent with the previously reported sense of benefit.

Without getting into further details about the differences between alumni from various types of institutions or indicating exactly what percentages of alumni have engaged in specific activities, I present next a list of alumni activities broadly grouped with respect to their relative frequency—beginning with activities which nearly all alumni said they had engaged in "during the past year" and ending with those in which very few alumni said they had engaged. The broad groupings of frequency are based on the responses of the total group of more than 8,000 college graduates. This is probably the most complete inventory that has yet been made of the involvement of college graduates in a wide range of civic and cultural affairs. These data have not previously been published.

Nearly all (80 percent or more) alumni said they did these things during the past year: (1) Community affairs—talked about local community problems with their friends; followed local events regularly in the newspaper; gave money to the community fund or chest or other local charity; voted in the last local election. (2) national and state politics—discussed political issues with their friends; listened to speeches, news specials, discussion programs, and so on about political issues on TV or radio weekly or monthly; followed state and national political events regularly in the newspaper; read magazine articles about state and national problems weekly or monthly; voted in the last national election; voted in the last state election. (3) Education—talked with their friends about the schools in the neighborhood; talked with a schoolteacher or other school official; read about education in the newspaper. (4) International—discussed international relations, foreign policy, the United Nations (U.N.), and so on with their friends; read newspapers or magazine articles dealing with international relations. (5) Music—listened attentively to radio music at home or in their car. (6) Drama—talked about movies, plays, TV dramas, and so on with their friends. (7) Religion—attended church services one or more times. (8) Science—watched special presentations about science on TV; read articles about new developments in scientific research in the newspapers or magazines.

Most alumni (50 to 79 percent) reported engaging in the following activities: (1) Community affairs—belonged to a community organization interested in civic affairs, such as the PTA, Chamber of Commerce, League of Women Voters, or a business or professional association; attended meetings of some local civic group; contributed time or money to some civic project, such as a playground, park, school, hospital, museum, or theater. (2) National and state politics—signed a petition, wrote a letter, card, or telegram concerned with some political issue. (3) Education—visited a local school; voted (or would vote) in favor of a bond issue or other proposition to provide more money for the public schools; gave money to a college or university. (4) Intercultural—talked with their friends about people and cultural events in other countries. (5) Art—talked about art with their friends; visited an art gallery or museum. (6) Literature—talked about new books with their friends; read book reviews in the newspapers or magazines at least once a month; bought books for their personal library; read one or more contemporary novels. (7) Music—bought phonograph records; talked about music with their friends. (8) Drama—watched TV dramas at least once a month; read theater or movie reviews in the newspapers or magazines at least once a month; attended one or more plays, either professional or amateur. (9) Religion—belonged to a church; contributed a regular sum of money to the church; read articles about church or religious activities in the newspapers or magazines; attended one or more church functions held during the week; did some volunteer work for their church; discussed ideas, practices, or problems of religion with their friends; observed religious rituals in their home (said grace before meals, lit candles on the Sabbath, and so on). (10) Science—talked about science with their friends.

A minority (from 20 to 49 percent) of the alumni reported that they did the following: (1) Community affairs—Had contact with a local official about some community problem; collected money, called on their neighbors, carried a petition, or engaged in some similar activity on behalf of a local community project; attended a public hearing about a local issue—such as zoning; held office in some local civic group or community organization. (2) National and state politics—read one or more books about politics; contributed money to some political cause or group; talked with an elected official about some problem (national or state). (3) Education—enrolled in a course offered by a college or university; attended one or more concerts or lectures at a college or university campus; attended one or more athletic events at a college or university; read one or more books about education. (4) Intercultural—saw one or more foreign movies; went to a concert, theater, or exhibition which featured the art, music, or drama of another country; corresponded with a citizen of another country; traveled in another country; entertained a visitor from another country; read one or more books by authors from another country; attended one or more meetings or lectures about other countries or about other racial or ethnic groups; participated in efforts to improve understanding between countries, races, or ethnic groups. (5) International—read one or more books about other countries or international relations; read U.N. publications or listened to U.N.-sponsored programs on radio or TV. (6) Art—read critiques or reviews of art shows or exhibits in the news-

papers or magazines; attended an exhibition of contemporary painting or sculpture; bought a painting or piece of sculpture. (7) Literature—read for personal interest (not business) at least one book a
month; read poetry. (8) Music—read reviews of musical per-
formances or new record releases in the newspapers or magazines;
attended one or more symphony, opera, or chamber music concerts;
attended one or more concerts of contemporary folk music, rock,
jazz, or the like; listened to some serious music by contemporary
composers; played a musical instrument. (9) Drama—went to the
movies at least once a month. (10) Religion—read one or more
books about religion. (11) Science—attended a scientific exhibit or
museum; read a new book about science; subscribed to a magazine
about science; attended a lecture or demonstration on some aspect
of science.

*And very few (19 percent or fewer) engaged in the following
activities:* (1) Community affairs—participated in a demonstration
or protest about a local issue. (2) National and state politics—attended meetings of a political club or group; did some volunteer or
paid work for a political party, participated in a public protest or
rally over some political issue; held a political or public office
(elected or appointed, full time or part time). (3) Intercultural—
attended a meeting at which a large majority of the participants
were of a racial background different from theirs. (4) International—
contributed time or money to some international group or project;
spoke to a civic group or club on international relations or foreign
policy; attended one or more meetings or lectures about international
affairs or foreign policy; wrote to a news publication or government
official in behalf of some legislation or U.S. policy regarding international relations; participated in a public demonstration for or
against some international issue. (5) Art—read one or more books
about art, artists, or art history; attended an art study group or
workshop; contributed money or time in support of some activity
related to art; did some creative painting or other art work. (6)
Literature—attended a lecture given by a novelist, critic, poet, or
playwright; belonged to a group which discussed books; wrote an
essay, story, play, poem, or something else for publication. (7)
Music—read one or more books about music, musicians, or music

history; contributed time or money to some local musical enterprise; participated in some vocal or instrumental group—choir, orchestra, or other group. (8) Drama—read one or more books about the theater, or a book of plays; belonged to a group which discussed contemporary drama; attended one or more plays by a contemporary dramatist; saw several movies that could be described as experimental or avant garde; contributed time or money in support of some local theatrical enterprise; participated in some drama activity —acted, danced, sang, worked on sets or costumes, made movies, and so on. (9) Science—attended meetings of a science study club or work group; carried out a scientific experiment, recorded scientific observations of things in the natural setting, or assembled and maintained a collection of scientific specimens; made some piece of scientific apparatus—such as a hi-fi component, photo-enlarger, or telescope.

Finally from the UCLA national study, I report some relevant information about occupation, income, the relation of current job to field of study in college, and general satisfaction with the college experience. First with respect to occupation, we found that 15 percent of the men identified themselves as being in a field which ordinarily required an advanced professional degree or doctorate, such as law, medicine, and college teaching. Another 42 percent described their occupations as being in some professional or technical field that ordinarily requires some training beyond college, typically a master's degree or other professional training, such as school-teaching, engineering, and accounting. An additional 31 percent identified their occupation as "managerial or executive." Thus 88 percent of the men graduates from 1950 are found in professional, managerial, or executive categories of employment. The median family income for the group was approximately $18,000. This compares with a census bureau estimate of $9,586 as the median family income for the nation as a whole at that time.

To get at their general attitude toward their undergraduate experience we asked the following question: "What is your present feeling about your college?" The responses were as follows: "strong attachment to it," 30 percent; "pleasantly nostalgic but no strong feeling," 50 percent; "more or less neutral," 16 percent; "generally negative," 3 percent; "thoroughly negative," 1 percent. No matter what type of college they had attended, the percentage of alumni expressing negative feelings was never greater than 6 percent.

Higher Education Research Institute (HERI) National Study of College Graduates and Employment

In the 1970s the focus of nationwide studies of college graduates again turned to questions of employment, and particularly to the relationship between college and work. One such survey was conducted by the Higher Education Research Institute (Solmon, Bisconti, and Ochsner, 1977). The data for that report came from the responses of 5,500 men and women who entered college as freshmen in 1961, subsequently attained a bachelor's degree, did not continue in school for any advanced degrees, and were working full time or had worked full time following their graduation from college. This group was a carefully selected subsample of more than 125,000 men and women who entered 248 bachelor's-degree-granting institutions as freshmen in the fall of 1961. The questionnaire to this subsample was mailed between November 1974 and March 1975. Altogether some 72 percent of those who received the questionnaire returned it.

With respect to the level of employment, 46 percent of the men and 78 percent of the women who were in full-time positions were classified by the authors as "professional, technical, and kindred." An additional 39 percent of the men and 11 percent of the women were described as managers or administrators. Thus 85 percent of the men and 89 percent of the women were employed at the two highest occupational levels.

With respect to income, there were major differences between the employed men and the employed women: 8 percent of the men and 36 percent of the women had incomes under $10,000; 46 percent of the men and 55 percent of the women had incomes between $10,000 and $17,000; and 46 percent of the men and 7 percent of the women had incomes of $17,000 and over. A rough estimate of the median income for those working full time would be $16,300 for the men and $11,800 for the women.

The following questions and responses concern various relationships between education and work. "How closely related is your job to your undergraduate major field?" Closely related—50 percent, somewhat related—24 percent, not related—26 percent. "How satisfied are you with your current job?" Very satisfied—53 percent, somewhat satisfied—41 percent, not at all satisfied—6 percent. "How useful was college in providing the knowledge and skills used in your current job?" Very useful—38 percent, somewhat —50 percent, not at all—12 percent. "How frequently do you use the content of courses in your undergraduate major field in your current job?" Almost always or frequently—48 percent, sometimes— 42 percent, rarely or never—10 percent.

Considering the fact that one fourth of the people said their current job was not related to their major field of study, it is particularly interesting to note that only 6 percent of the group said they were not at all satisfied with their current job, only 12 percent said college was not at all useful in providing the knowledge and skills they used in their current job, and only 10 percent said they rarely or never used the content of the courses in their major field in their current job.

These relationships vary considerably, of course, depending on what the students' major field had been and on what their present line of work was. Here are a few examples from the results of the survey: two thirds of those who had majored in education and somewhat more than half of those who had majored in the natural sciences or in business said that they frequently or almost always used the content of courses from their major field in their current work. This level of frequency was also indicated by half of those who had majored in English and half of those who had majored in engineering. Among arts and humanities majors, 41 percent said they almost always or frequently used such knowledge in their current work; and that was also true of 39 percent of those who had majored in mathematics. Among economics majors and social science majors the corresponding proportions were one third and one fourth.

Looking at the relation between education and work from a different perspective, one finds that the connection is very close or very weak depending on the particular occupation. More than 80 percent of the graduates who were teachers or whose work was described as in "allied health fields" reported that their job was closely related to their undergraduate major field. Three fourths of the accountants and two thirds of the engineers also indicated that their jobs were closely related to their undergraduate major. In contrast to these relatively strong relationships, only a minority of those whose current occupations were in business and in administration felt that their work was closely related to their undergraduate major field. The percentages were as follows: 39 percent for business administrators; 35 percent for business owners; 24 percent for salespersons; and 18 percent for occupations described as "middle administrator."

The 1976
Associated Colleges of the Midwest (ACM)
Survey of Liberal Arts Graduates

Early in 1976 a questionnaire was sent to all graduates of the class of 1975 from eleven liberal arts colleges in the Midwest and to a sample of their graduates from the classes of 1970, 1965, and 1960 (Wishart and Rossmann, 1977). There were 3,000 in the most recent graduating class, and a sample of 3,000 from the earlier classes. Responses were received from 61 percent of the 1975 graduates and 51 percent of the earlier graduates. Although this is not a nationwide survey, it has special significance for two reasons: the eleven colleges are all liberal arts colleges, deeply committed to the importance and value of liberal education, and offering little direct vocational training; and the graduates of 1975 entered the labor market at a difficult time.

From many accounts in the national media one would suppose that these 1975 graduates were an unhappy and unfortunate group, starting life after college with two strikes against them. Nearly all of them, 85 percent, had majored in traditional liberal arts subjects; and thus only 15 percent had majored in a field directly related to an occupation, such as education, business, or nursing. Moreover, when they graduated, the national unemployment average was 7.5 percent, and a discouraging 13 percent for those twenty to twenty-four years old.

This study of these recent liberal arts graduates, however, reveals a very different picture. Six to nine months after graduation, when they received the questionnaire, only 4 percent of the men

and 5 percent of the women were unemployed and seeking employment. The others had full-time jobs (48 percent of the men and
56 percent of the women), were in graduate or professional school
(36 percent of the men and 22 percent of the women), or were
engaged in some other activity, such as household duties, military
service, Peace Corps service, travel, or part-time work. Those working full time had good jobs. For 62 percent of the men and 69 percent of the women the jobs were classified as professional, technical,
managerial, or administrative. About the same proportions thought
their jobs had definite or possible career potential. Relatively few
of them, 14 percent of the men and 12 percent of the women, said
they did not like their jobs.

Asked to evaluate their college experiences *in terms of employability only,* 85 percent of the men and 83 percent of the women
said they were generally satisfied with their college. Despite the fact
that somewhat more than a third were in jobs not related to their
major field of study, only 8 percent said they were dissatisfied with
their undergraduate major, again *in terms of employability only.*

A particularly interesting aspect of this alumni survey, because it rather clearly suggests why and how liberal education is so
relevant to success and careers, is the series of comparisons between
what the alumni judged to be important for success and what they
felt college had provided. For instance, 93 percent of the 1975
graduates said "acquiring new skills on my own" was necessary for
success, and 92 percent rated their college as effective or somewhat
effective in helping them develop this competence. The respective
percentages for the five other top-rated abilities were as follows:
choosing between alternative courses of action—90 and 89 percent;
communicating orally effectively—89 and 81 percent; thinking
analytically—87 and 96 percent; functioning as a team member—
85 and 79 percent; and being sensitive to the feelings and perceptions of others—84 and 86 percent. And every other kind of competence identified as necessary for success was also identified as one
that college helped them to develop.

The full report of the ACM study includes comparisons
between the recent graduates and those who had graduated five,
ten, and fifteen years earlier. Basically, the comparisons show that
among those who have been out of college for five to fifteen years
there are greater proportions employed at the top occupational

levels, larger proportions who are satisfied with their jobs, much higher income levels, equal satisfaction with the college experience, and equally positive judgments about the effectiveness of college in developing the abilities necessary for success.

All the Studies Compared:
College Graduates from the 1930s to the 1970s

To summarize the major results from all the alumni studies I have described, I have selected various topics that have been included in several of them and briefly reported the responses so that one can see at a glance the general consistency in what has been learned. One must remember that each study has its own unique sample of respondents, that the data from some surveys have come from fairly recent alumni while others have come from alumni who have been out of college for ten to twenty years or more. So the results from the several studies are not directly comparable. Yet despite these obvious differences, differences that necessarily would produce variations in the results, it is nevertheless instructive to line them up and see whether they tell a roughly similar story. The following brief labels will be used to identify the studies:

- Minnesota = Survey in 1937 of 6,000 Minnesota graduates from the years 1928 to 1936
- Minnesota GC = Minnesota General College Survey, made in 1937–38, of 951 former Minnesota students who entered the university in 1924–25 and 1928–29
- USOE = Survey of 45,000 graduates of 31 universities during the years 1928–1935, made in 1936
- *Time* = Survey of 9,000 living college graduates from 1,000 colleges, made in 1947
- Syracuse = Survey of 2,000 Syracuse graduates of 1947, 1942, 1937, 1932, 1927, made in 1948
- Calvert = Survey of 11,000 men graduates in liberal arts from 100 colleges, five, ten, and fifteen years after graduation, made in 1963
- NORC = Survey of 5,000 graduates of 1961 from 135 colleges, made in 1968
- UCLA = Survey of 8,000 graduates of 1950 from 74 colleges, made in 1969

- HERI = Survey of 5,500 graduates from 248 colleges who entered college in 1961, made in 1974–75
- ACM = Survey done in 1976 of 3,300 graduates from 11 liberal arts colleges—half of them less than one year after graduation, the other half five, ten, and fifteen years after graduation.

Here, then, are the summaries of results:

Occupational Level of Men Graduates

Minnesota	79% at professional or managerial level
Minnesota GC	77% at professional or managerial level
USOE	63% at professional level
Time	84% at professional or managerial level
Syracuse	70% at professional or managerial level
Calvert	67% at professional or managerial level
NORC	90% at professional or managerial level
UCLA	88% at professional or managerial level
HERI	85% at professional or managerial level
ACM	62% at professional or managerial level less than one year after graduation
	90% at professional or managerial level five, ten, and fifteen years after graduation

Thus men graduates, from the 1920s to the 1970s, have typically found employment in the two highest occupational categories. The definitions of these categories have changed—that is, more lines of work are called professional today than were called that forty years ago—but in relative terms graduates continue in overwhelming numbers to work at the top levels.

Income

Minnesota	$2500 in 1936 for men out of college seven to eight years
Minnesota GC	$2400 in 1937 for men out of college seven or eight years
USOE	$2400 in 1936 for men out of college for eight years

	(The U.S. median family income in 1935–36 was $1025.)
Time	$5400 median family income in 1947—one third out of college for less than eight years; one third out of college from eight to sixteen years; and one third out of college for more than sixteen years
Syracuse	$5300 median family income in 1948—one third out of college for one year; two thirds out of college from six to twenty-one years
	(The U.S. median family income in 1946 was $2981.)
Calvert	$8000 median salary in 1963 for men five years out of college
	$10,500 median salary in 1963 for men ten years out of college
	$13,000 median salary in 1963 for men fifteen years out of college
	(The U.S. median family income in 1963 was $6265.)
UCLA	$18,000 median family income in 1969 for graduates eighteen years out of college
	(The U.S. median family income in 1969 was $9586.)
HERI	$16,300 median income in 1974 for men graduates about eight or nine years out of college and who had no education beyond the bachelor's degree
	(The U.S. median family income in 1974 was $14,082.)
ACM	$8900 median income for men graduates less than one year out of college
	$19,400 for men graduates five, ten, and fifteen years out of college combined

The U.S. median family income figures all come from the U.S. Bureau of the Census, *Statistical Abstract of the United States.* The surveys of college graduates made in the 1930s, the 1940s, and the 1960s all show incomes, whether individual or family incomes, that are roughly twice as much as the U.S. median family income at those times. The data for 1974 in the HERI study are not comparable to those from the other surveys and therefore need further interpretation: first, by excluding graduates who continued their training in graduate and professional school, the HERI study excludes those who enter the highest-paying professions, such as medicine and law; second, over the past few years there has been a large increase in the number of two-income families, especially among college graduates; and third, the proportion of young adults today who are college graduates is larger than it was in the 1960s, and much larger than it was in the 1940s and 1930s, thus composing a larger share of the U.S. median family income figures. Making a reasonable allowance for these three factors, my guess is that a better estimate of the median family income of college graduates in 1974 would be about $21,000, or at least 50 percent higher than the U.S. median. Moreover, this comparison includes only fairly recent graduates who have been in the labor force for a short time. Clearly, the income difference between graduates and the population in general is still very great.

Job Satisfaction

Minnesota GC	On a scale from 4 to 28, the mean score of graduates was 21, typified by the statement "I like it"
Calvert	69% like their work very much; 22% fairly much; and 6% dislike it slightly or greatly
HERI	53% very satisfied; 41% somewhat satisfied; 6% not satisfied
ACM	For graduates less than one year out of college: 36% enthusiastic, 34% like it, 18% neutral, 13% don't like it
	For graduates five, ten, and fifteen years out of college, combined: 58% enthusiastic, 30% like it, 8% neutral, 5% don't like it

Very few college graduates dislike or are not satisfied with their jobs.

Relationship of Job to Major Field of Study

Minnesota 67% men, 75% women in same field (first job) (dropped to about 60% in the Depression)

80% to 90% in same or related field (first job)

USOE 70%+ in same or closely related field (first job) (dropped to 52% in the Depression)

61% to 69% men, 53% to 61% women in same or closely related field (present job)

Time 56% men, 44% women in same field (present job)

Syracuse 77% men, 81% women in same or related field (first job)

75% men, 62% women in same or related field (present job)

HERI 50% in closely related field (present job)

74% in closely or somewhat related field (present job)

ACM For graduates less than one year out of college: 58% men, 68% women in closely or somewhat related field

For graduates five, ten, and fifteen years out of college combined: 75% men, 75% women in closely or somewhat related field

Most college graduates, then, generally two thirds to three fourths, work in fields that are similar to their major field of study in college.

Vocational Relevance of College

Time 73% college helped a lot in present job

25% college helped some

2% college helped not at all

Syracuse 57% college helped much in preparing for a vocation

32% college helped some

9% college helped little or not at all

Calvert	73% received good preparation for their vocational life
NORC	86% general college training prepared them very or moderately well for current job
UCLA	64% received very much or quite a bit of benefit in background and specialization for further education in some professional, scientific, or scholarly field
	43% received very much or quite a bit of benefit in vocational training—skills and techniques directly applicable to a job
HERI	38% said college was very useful in providing knowledge and skills used in current job
	50% said college was somewhat useful
	12% said college was not at all useful
	48% said they almost always or frequently use content of major courses in their work
	42% said sometimes
	10% said rarely
ACM	84% of graduates less than one year out of college said that "in terms of employability alone" they were satisfied with their undergraduate college; among older graduates it was 90%
	90%, approximately, of all groups said that "in terms of employability alone" they were satisfied with their undergraduate major

For most alumni the vocational relevance of what they studied in college turns out to be fairly substantial—two thirds to nine tenths citing at least some or moderate relevance, and from one third to three fourths giving such responses as "much," "a lot," and "very useful." This degree of relationship, as well as the relationship noted earlier between present job and major field, is especially interesting because roughly half of the alumni in the studies by Calvert and by HERI said they did not choose their vocations until after graduation.

Satisfaction with College and Attitude toward College

Time   84% would go back to same college

Syracuse   88% would recommend Syracuse to a close friend

Calvert   57% would go back to same college

                29% not sure

                14% would not

NORC   27% feel strong attachment to their college

                59% like it but not strongly

                10% mixed feelings

                 3% don't like it much, but not strongly

                 1% thoroughly dislike it

UCLA   30% feel strong attachment

                50% pleasant feelings, but not strong

                16% more or less neutral

                 3% generally negative

                 1% thoroughly negative

Clearly, very few alumni have negative attitudes toward the college they attended.

Political Activities

Minnesota GC   80%+ voted in last national election (1936)

                During the past year:

                about 30% signed a petition

                about 20% campaigned for a candidate

                about 20% wrote a letter to a public official

                about 20% attended meetings of a political club

Time   79% voted in the last national election (1944)

                During the past year:

                30% signed a petition

                23% wrote to a public official

                17% contributed money to some political cause or group

Syracuse   69% voted in the last national election (1944)

                During the past year:

29% signed a petition

20% wrote to a public official

13% contributed money to some political cause or group

UCLA

80%+ voted in the last national election (1968) During the past year:

50 to 79% signed a petition, or wrote a letter, card, or telegram

20 to 49% talked with an elected official about some problem

20 to 49% contributed money to some political cause or group

By way of comparison, we might note the U.S. Bureau of the Census (1977) report that 85 percent of college graduates voted in 1968, as did 75 percent of high school graduates, 64 percent of those who had some high school, and 53 percent of those who did not complete school beyond the eighth grade.

Cultural Activities and Interests

Minnesota GC

(graduates only)

53% men, 86% women read books frequently or fairly often

17% men, 37% women attend concerts frequently or fairly often

36% men, 41% women go to the theater frequently or fairly often

22% men, 47% women use public library frequently or fairly often

6% men, 20% women visit museums and art galleries frequently or fairly often

Syracuse

During the past year:

55% attended one or more concerts

43% visited an art gallery or museum

28% visited a science museum or exhibition

Calvert

During the past year:

66% attended two or more theatrical productions

60% visited an art museum

43% read more than five books of fiction

36% read more than five books of nonfiction

36% attended two or more operas or symphony concerts

NORC 81% read nonfiction frequently or occasionally

66% read fiction frequently or occasionally

57% go to plays frequently or occasionally

56% go to museums or art galleries frequently or occasionally

41% go to concerts frequently or occasionally

UCLA During the past year:

50 to 79% visited an art gallery or museum

50 to 79% attended one or more plays

20 to 49% attended one or more concerts (symphony, opera, chamber music)

Critical Thinking and Expression

Syracuse 90% received much or some help in critical thinking

83% received much or some help in writing clearly and effectively

81% received much or some help in speaking easily and well

Calvert 69% agreed that college gave them good training in how to express their ideas clearly

NORC 87% said college affected them greatly or somewhat in developing their abilities to think and express themselves

UCLA 72% received very much or quite a bit of benefit in critical thinking

63% received very much or quite a bit of benefit in writing or speaking clearly, correctly, and effectively

ACM 96% of all graduates combined said college was effective or somewhat effective in developing their ability to think analytically

85% said it was effective or somewhat effective in developing their capacity to write well

82% said it was effective or somewhat effective in developing their ability to communicate orally effectively

Breadth of Knowledge

Syracuse   79% received much or some help in understanding world issues and social, political, and economic problems

77% received much or some help in developing an understanding and enjoyment of literature

62% received much or some help in understanding scientific developments and processes

58% received much or some help in developing an understanding and enjoyment of art and music

Calvert   80% said college provided a broad fund of knowledge about different fields

UCLA   77% said college affected them greatly or somewhat in giving them a broad knowledge of the arts and sciences

NORC   79% received very much or quite a bit of benefit in learning vocabulary, terminology, and facts in various fields of knowledge

Interpersonal Skills

Syracuse   89% received much or some help in developing social competence

91% received much or some help in understanding other people

Calvert   72% said college developed their ability to get along with different types of people

53% said college developed their social poise

NORC   68% said college affected them greatly or
                      somewhat in helping them learn how to
                      get along with others
UCLA   61% received very much or quite a bit of
                      benefit in social development—experience
                      or skill in relating to other people
                      56% received very much or quite a bit of
                      benefit in tolerance and understanding of
                      other people and their values
ACM   85% of all graduates said college was effective
                      or somewhat effective in developing their
                      sensitivity to the feelings and perceptions
                      of others
                      82% of all graduates said college was effective
                      or somewhat effective in developing their
                      competence to function as a team member

Values, Goals, Philosophy

Syracuse   79% received much or some help in under-
                      standing the meaning and values in life
                      73% received much or some help in develop-
                      ing a personal philosophy of life
Calvert   68% said college developed their moral capaci-
                      ties, ethical standards, and values
NORC   64% said college affected them greatly or
                      somewhat in helping them formulate the
                      values and goals of their life
UCLA   64% received very much or quite a bit of
                      benefit in awareness of different philos-
                      ophies, cultures, and ways of life
ACM   80% of all graduates said college was effective
                      or somewhat effective in developing their
                      competence to cope with moral and ethical
                      issues

Do college graduates have good jobs? Yes.
Do college graduates have good incomes? Yes.

Do college graduates like their jobs? Yes.

Do college graduates think their education was relevant for their jobs? Yes.

Do college graduates feel satisfied about the college they attended? Yes.

Do college graduates participate actively in political, civic, and cultural enterprises? Yes.

Do college graduates think their education developed their ability to think critically and express themselves clearly? Yes.

Do college graduates think their education gave them breadth of knowledge about various fields? Yes.

Do college graduates think their education helped them in understanding and relating to other people? Yes.

Do college graduates think their education helped them develop and clarify their values and goals? Yes.

These simple yes answers are based on evidence from alumni of many colleges, alumni who have been out of college for different lengths of time, and from surveys from the 1930s to the 1970s. If consistency is cause for confidence, we can be confident in what we know about college graduates.

Graduates and Their Knowledge

Our knowledge about college graduates from the alumni surveys I have reported is fairly extensive, and the results have been fairly consistent over several decades; but these studies have told us very little about *their* knowledge. If we agree that the transmission of knowledge is one of the main purposes of higher education, we surely ought to know something about what knowledge is possessed by people who have graduated from college. Giving a battery of achievement tests to a national sample of college graduates is not feasible and perhaps never will be. Despite this obstacle we do in fact have a lot of information about what college graduates know. The information comes from what are commonly called public opinion polls, which, in addition to opinion questions, sometimes include knowledge questions, such as, Will you tell me what the term *filibuster* means to you? What is the population of the United States? Who wrote *War and Peace?* What are the names of the senators from this state? Which planet is nearest the sun? Can you tell me who these people are or what they do? (Persons who have been named over the years include Dean Rusk, Casey Stengel, Earl Warren, J. Edgar Hoover, George Meany, John Glenn, Nelson Rockefeller, and Elizabeth Taylor.) Have you heard or read about fluoridating public water supplies?

From fifty-one national sample surveys of adults over two decades, 1949 to 1971, conducted by the Gallup Poll, the National Opinion Research Center at the University of Chicago, and the Survey Research Center at the University of Michigan, 250 questions on specific knowledge were asked. Of the 77,000 adults included in these surveys, 8,400 were college graduates: their knowledge, compared with that possessed by adults who had lesser amounts of formal schooling—namely, high school and elementary school graduates—has been analyzed and reported in a book whose title, *The Enduring Effects of Education,* reveals the basic conclusion from the analyses (Hyman, Wright, and Reed, 1975).

Most of the knowledge questions in these national surveys were about public affairs, both foreign and domestic, and about important people in the news of the day. Answers to such questions could not have been learned in school. The events had not yet happened. Knowing the answers to these questions thus reflects a receptivity to knowledge about the world in which one is living. There were 140 questions of this type. In addition there were 88 questions which could be regarded as requiring academic knowledge or knowledge probably acquired in school. Most of these items elicited simple factual knowledge about geography, history, the humanities, and the sciences. Eleven questions were about popular culture—heroes and idols from the world of sport, movies, space, glamour. And eleven questions probed the respondent's knowledge of the tools and duties in different occupations, both white collar and blue collar. What we have in these surveys, then, are tests of the knowledge possessed by national samples of the adult population—academic knowledge, knowledge of people and events in the news, and some knowledge of popular culture and different occupations.

In analyzing the results of these tests, the authors have looked at four different periods—the early 1950s, the late 1950s, the early 1960s, and the late 1960s. In each period, and in all surveys, they looked further at the results from four different age groups—ages twenty-five to thirty-six, thirty-seven to forty-eight, forty-nine to sixty, and sixty-one to seventy-two. Within every period and every age group the percentage of college graduates who know the answers was compared with the percentage of adult high school graduates and elementary school graduates. Thus sixteen basic groups—four age groups by four time periods—formed the heart of the comparisons of the differences in knowledge of adults at three educational levels.

With such rare exceptions that one needs a magnifying glass and a proofreader's eye to find them, the percentage of adults who know the answers is highest among those who graduated from college, next highest among those who graduated from high school, and lowest among those who had only an elementary school education. This is true of all age groups and of all time periods. The differences persist even when the different groups are controlled or equated in terms of sex, religion, social class origins, and socioeconomic status. In short, what is revealed by the analyses is the enduring effect of education. The differences between the educational levels are major, as the selected examples shown in Table 18 reveal. Over the entire set of questions from all the surveys, the typical or average percentage of college graduates knowing the correct answer was 80 percent; for high school graduates it was 62 percent; and for adults with an elementary school education it was 38 percent. The authors of the report summarize their conclusions as follows: "Many and varied measurements over thousands of adults, drawn from a long series of national samples and thus representing the students taught in all the nation's schools and colleges over a long period, lead us to conclude that education produces large, pervasive, and enduring effects on knowledge and receptivity to knowledge (Hyman, Wright, and Reed, 1975, p. 109).

Two final items from the report are noted because they relate to information from some of the alumni studies described previously. In five of the national surveys, the adults were asked about their reading of magazines. Combining the responses from these different surveys and for the different age groups, one finds that the proportions who said they read one or more magazines regularly were 92 percent among college graduates, 78 percent among high school

Table 18. Examples of differences in knowledge related to education—from national surveys of the adult population

| | Percentages Knowing the Correct Answer | | | | | |
| | Youngest Age Group 25 to 36 | | | Oldest Age Group 61 to 72 | | |
	Elem	HS	Coll	Elem	HS	Coll
From surveys in the early 1950s						
Know Earl Warren	36	69	88	45	68	100
Know Tito	20	42	82	24	57	75
Know Freud	4	27	73	1	25	83
Know Aristotle	4	45	90	8	50	100
Know "filibuster"	28	64	89	30	51	82
Heard of NATO	28	41	90	27	62	100
Can locate Iran	15	29	45	9	25	80
From surveys in the early 1960s						
Know Goldwater	26	59	92	49	68	87
Know J. Edgar Hoover	38	89	100	69	88	100
Heard of nuclear test ban	65	72	99	61	72	92
Know electoral college	3	46	83	31	45	85
Know five or more cabinet positions	0	31	80	16	29	75

Source: Hyman, Wright, and Reed, 1975; from Appendix B, tables 1.1, 1.4, 1.5, 1.8, 3.1, 3.4, and 3.5.

graduates, and 43 percent among adults with an elementary school education. Also in five national surveys, adults were asked whether they had read a book during the past year. Answering yes to this question were 85 percent of the college graduates, 60 percent of the high school graduates, and 28 percent of those with an elementary school education.

Alumni Surveys for the Future

As I pointed out earlier, in the field of college student achievement testing, the need is first to encourage more use of the excellent measures that already exist and second to encourage the development of new kinds of measures. But in the study of college graduates we need to devise standardized measures in a field where none now exists. Each new investigator of alumni has devised his own new questionnaire. Some efforts toward greater commonality in measurement and content would contribute to firmer generalizations in the future about the subsequent status of college graduates.

Alumni questionnaires used in major surveys over the past forty years have had some similarity in content. As noted, several have been concerned with occupational and financial status, job satisfaction, the relation of jobs to major fields of study in college, and other associations between education and work. Several have analyzed the alumni's involvement in a variety of civic and cultural activities. Several have inquired about their satisfaction with various aspects of their college experience and with the particular college they attended. And several have had content related to the alumni's opinions about the extent to which college influenced them in various ways and provided them with knowledge and skills and experiences which they regard as benefits. Rarely, however, has this general similarity in content been expressed by identical questions with identical response categories.

The task of developing a systematic body of content for alumni surveys is basically no different from the task of developing a systematic body of content for achievement tests. One first needs a test blueprint. What is to be measured? What information from and about alumni is relevant to the purposes of higher education? What evidence is pertinent for assessing the long-range or residual benefits, or detriments, of the college experience? Just as makers of achievement tests must decide on the subject matter to be covered—the physical, natural, and social sciences, humanities and arts, for example, and more specific content within those broad categories—so makers of alumni questionnaires must decide on the content appropriate for that purpose.

Makers of achievement tests have relatively clear guides for selecting appropriate content—textbooks, course syllabi, meetings with professors who teach the subject. But what are the guidelines for alumni surveys? There are no comparable references. One can of course look at typical statements of objectives. Although such statements generally refer to undergraduate education, many of them are also relevant to college graduates: for example, critical thinking, clarification of one's philosophy, ethics, and morality, responsible citizenship, esthetic sensitivity, tolerance, appreciation of other cultures, self-directed learning, understanding science and technology, vocational training, and breadth of knowledge. Or one could look at other often-used guidelines, such as the relevance of higher education to occupations and careers, or the monetary returns on the investment in higher education.

Whatever the proper guidelines may be, one needs to set forth their rationale and to develop the content of a "test battery for alumni" accordingly. I do not think the result of such efforts to devise a valid blueprint can be translated into a single questionnaire. I am inclined to believe that a set of instruments would be necessary and more useful. In any case, I surely do not think that a miscellaneous assortment of questions used by one researcher in one study will ever be widely adopted by other researchers. What is needed is a program of collaboration resulting in some consensus. That is the way achievement test batteries are made. It is also the way alumni survey instruments should be made.

Here are some tentative thoughts about the kinds of content that are important in studying college graduates. First, I should think that one would want to know something about the knowledge possessed by alumni. The instrument used might be a brief counterpart of undergraduate achievement tests, emphasizing concepts and generalizations rather than specific facts or vocabulary in the major academic disciplines. Or it might evaluate knowledge related to major social issues such as energy. Or it might be a current affairs test, periodically revised. In any case, the measurement of knowledge is the most conspicuously neglected item in past studies of college graduates. Second, I should think that one would look for evidence of personal achievement. This might be revealed by occupational success and satisfaction (whatever the occupation), by effective and satisfying relationships with other people, by general life satisfaction, and so on. Third, I should think that a study of college graduates would look for evidence of intellectual interests and habits such as might be revealed by continuing education (learning new things), by habits of critical thinking, reason, curiosity, and openness to inquiry. Fourth, since college graduates are both consumers of and contributors to the community and the culture in which they live, I think one should look for evidence of the quality of their consumption (standards of judgment and taste) and the quality of their contribution (involvement in and interpretation of the community and the culture). There are several major areas of consumption and contribution in which the standards and the involvement of college graduates may be particularly relevant to the basic aims of higher education: exemplifying a knowledge and concern about the role of science and technology in human affairs; exemplifying a concern for the quality of government, civic affairs, the functioning of organizations and groups: exemplifying interest in, support for, and pleasure in cultural and esthetic affairs and discriminating taste (art, music, drama, literature, and the like); and exemplifying broad persepectives (historical, philosophical, intercultural, and ethical) in one's thought and action about critical issues and choices. Fifth, I should think one would want to know how college graduates evaluate their own educational experience and how they view higher education as a major social institution. And sixth, because large numbers of students go on to graduate and professional school after completing their bachelor's degree, special attention should be given to that subsequent experience, particularly as it relates to careers. The evaluation of the undergraduate experience only is no longer sufficient for alumni studies. These tentative suggestions might provide an initial framework for more extensive and specific thoughts about the relevant content for new studies of college alumni, leading ultimately to some agreement about a battery of instruments which might be widely adopted and thereby lift alumni surveys to a higher plane of usefulness.

There is one current effort to produce a standard questionnaire for recent alumni, an effort initiated by the National Center for Higher Education Management Systems (NCHEMS, 1979). The questionnaire they have produced is brief, objective, and easy to use. It is available not only from NCHEMS but also from the College Entrance Examination Board. The questionnaire is intended to be answered about six months to a year after leaving school. Basically, it addresses three topics. First, it asks the respondents a few questions about further education: Are they enrolled in another degree program? How well did the school prepare them for this new program? What's the highest degree they intend to complete? Second, it asks about their first full-time job since graduation: How long did it take them to find the job? How did they learn about it? Was the job related to their college major program, and if not, why not? How well did college prepare them for the job? And what was the starting salary? Third, it inquires about various goals of college education—academic goals, career goals, social and cultural goals, personal development goals—by asking them first to check the ones that were important to them when they attended college and second to indicate whether they think they have achieved or are achieving the goals.

This is useful, albeit very limited, information for a college to have. It does not, however, deal with the range and depth of inquiry I have suggested in thinking about a "test battery for alumni." In fact, it includes nothing about knowledge, or personal achievement, or intellectual interests, or cultural interests, or values, or any other fundamental goals of higher education. As for any evaluation of college, it asks only two simple questions: How well did our college prepare you for additional college work? How well did our college prepare you for your first job? The NCHEMS questionnaire is not really addressed to college graduates; it is addressed to anyone who has recently left school, even though their attendance had been for as little as one term. In this sense, it is not an "alumni" questionnaire; and it does not represent a useful new direction for the study of college graduates. Its utility is mainly in the encouragement it may give to institutions to find out at least a little something about the students who have recently left.

The more penetrating inquiry I would like to see, and which I believe is the significant new direction for alumni surveys, is perhaps best regarded as appropriate for alumni ten to fifteen to twenty years after graduation. This extended period is surely needed if we are to learn more about the enduring influence of higher education in people's lives and about the role of college graduates in our society.

III

Achievement
by Colleges:
Studies of Institutions

Colleges and universities are in their very nature introspective, self-conscious, and self-critical. Indeed, among all the major institutions in our society, it may well be that colleges and universities have been the most thoroughly and repeatedly studied—more so than hospitals or prisons, government bureaus or military organizations, business or industrial organizations, churches or charitable organizations. By "studied," I mean systematically, objectively, and comparatively. I also mean studied as institutions—their purposes and programs, physical plant and facilities, organization and administration, governance and finance, students and faculty, and other institutional features. When sociologists, economists, industrial psychologists, administrators, and others say that colleges and universities have not been studied, or at best have been just recently subjected to scrutiny, they are mistaken. And yet despite all these analyses it may still be true that colleges and universities, as organizations, are less well understood than other types of institutions. We shall see, in fact, that our understanding of the connections between organizational characteristics and organizational achievement is not nearly as clear as it should be.

As in the two previous sections, my intent here is to select a few landmark lines of inquiry and specific studies as illustrations of the vast volume of examinations that have been made of colleges and universities. The major types of inquiries do not follow one another in chronological sequence. And thus although one could describe the types of studies made during each successive decade, I have chosen to emphasize types rather than sequence, since types and times both overlap.

There are two kinds of inquiry—internal and external. Internal studies are, or should be, introspective and self-critical. They are concerned with how the institution works, given its particular set of people, programs, purposes, and resources. They are also evaluative or self-critical, concerned with how well the institution works. External studies are comparative or interinstitutional. Their intent is usually to identify differences between institutions, to build a data base against which to examine and compare variations in the practices, purposes, and achievements of different types of institutions, or of institutions within a state, region, or larger territory.

Self-Studies and Institutional Research

Self-studies are analyses of a particular institution made by people at the institution, and institutional research has come to be the label attached to offices within colleges and universities whose continuing role is to evaluate local programs and assemble relevant information for planning programs and allocating resources. The establishment of such offices on university campuses has a long history. Before 1930, for example, various organizations, sometimes called the Bureau of Institutional Research or Bureau of Educational Research, were created at such major institutions as the University of Illinois, Ohio State, Minnesota, and Purdue.

The Minnesota group, established in 1924, was called the Committee on Educational Research. The scope of its inquiries is well illustrated by a brief reference to the Biennial Reports of its work for 1938–1940 and 1940–1942. During that four-year period, the results of thirty special studies were reported. Among them were a survey of what happens to high school graduates, a study of the reactions of freshmen throughout Minnesota to their first year of college, a study of student retention and drop-out, a comparison of different methods of instruction in certain fields, evaluations of some new programs in the General College of the University of Minnesota, and studies on predicting students' success in various schools and colleges of the university. They also included a university-wide faculty load study and a university curriculum survey. There were also a number of studies involving the construction and use of comprehensive examinations in various schools and colleges of the university. In 1948 the Committee on Educational Research was renamed the Bureau of Institutional Research. Later the activities of the Bureau were merged in a more general administrative office concerned with university planning and budgeting. The Minnesota Bureau of Institutional Research published a book reporting major inquiries undertaken during the decade 1942 to 1952 (Eckert and Keller, 1954). This report is probably the best single example of the nature of institutional research at that time.

Another early example of institutional research was the establishment at Purdue, in 1925, of an organization called the Division of Educational Reference. The Division subsequently issued the results of many studies of education at Purdue, under the general heading of Studies in Higher Education. By 1960, more than a hundred bulletins had been published by the Division. Their topics have included the prediction of students' success, students' ratings of courses and instructors, students' attitudes and satisfactions, special programs such as freshmen orientation, remedial programs, and extracurricular activities.

Paul Dressel edited a book (1954) in which the results of evaluation studies at several institutions were reported, including Syracuse, Minnesota, Antioch, Pennsylvania College for Women, San Francisco State, Stephens College, Chicago City Junior College, the University of Florida, Western Washington College of Education, Purdue, Drake University, the University of Chicago, and the Basic College at Michigan State. Many of these evaluations were concerned with developing achievement tests and other measures of general education outcomes. Indeed, one emphasis in the early development of institutional research was on improving examinations.

The rapid spread of institutional research in the decade of the 1950s, following World War II, led the American Association of Land Grant Colleges and State Universities and the State Universities Association to survey the amount and scope of institutional research in those institutions. The survey (Stickler, 1959) involved ninety-three institutions, of which fifty-nine had made a comprehensive self-study since the end of World War II: nine out of ten were engaged in institutional research of some character and to some extent, although in the period January 1954 to July 1959 this activity was not highly centralized or well organized in most places.

The further rapid growth of institutional research is well illustrated by the founding, in the 1960s, of the Association for Institutional Research. In its 1977–78 directory, which lists more than 1300 members, more than 250 are called Director, Institutional Research, and more than 100 others have a somewhat similar title. If one assumes that the existence of a person with such a title on a particular campus means that this campus has more than a single individual handling such matters, and that the director is a full-time staff member, then in comparison with Stickler's survey in 1959, which showed that only 18 of 93 institutions had a full-time coordinator, the growth has certainly been dramatic.

In the early development of what I have called institutional research, the emphasis tended to be mainly on educational research—that is, on evaluating curricula, assessing students' achievement, predicting their success, comparing different teaching methods, and studying students' attitudes and satisfaction. Since then, the emphasis has gradually shifted toward institutional accounting and the collection of data specifically relevant for institutional planning and budgeting. This shift coincided to a considerable extent with the advent of computers. With the basic data on computer tape, the institutional research offices were able to produce reports monitoring the flow of students through the institution by departments, by years, by credit hours, and other classifications, together with data on budgets and costs, faculty salaries, and so on, so that the cost of instruction per credit hour and similar indexes could be readily produced. And also, periodic surveys of faculty teaching loads, of library costs per student, and many other aspects of institutional functioning were gradually centralized in an office of institutional research. More detailed and precise procedures and definitions were developed for computing such indexes and for making other studies on such subjects as space utilization, class size, and teaching load. Today almost all institutions of moderate to large size have some kind of institutional research office. Indeed, such an office has come to be viewed as a necessity.

Insofar as institutional research offices concern themselves with more than institutional accounting and budgetary matters, dealing also with the goals of the institution, the achievement of students, the effectiveness of instruction and similar educational as opposed to financial or administrative topics, they can be regarded as engaged in continuing institutional self-study. In most cases, however, the continuing operations of an institutional research office differ from a self-study, which gives relatively more attention to educational goals and outcomes and to the cooperative involvement of the faculty.

When the General College of the University of Minnesota was established in 1932, it promptly engaged in some very intensive self-analysis. The curriculum of the college was quite different from the traditional liberal arts curriculum; the students were quite different from other University of Minnesota students; the purpose of the institution within the University was frankly experimental; and the need for thorough study of its program and practices was clear. Consequently, a great deal of attention was given from the outset to specifying the college's objectives and the objectives of courses within the college. The results of the self-studies, which extended over a period of several years, were ultimately published in four volumes (Pace, 1941; Williams, 1943; Spafford and others, 1943; and Eckert, 1943). The last of those volumes, entitled *Outcomes of General Education,* provided a systematic appraisal of the General College program.

The typical focus of self-studies on institutional aims and purposes is further illustrated by a program initiated by the Fund for the Advancement of Education in the years following World War II. The Fund, primarily concerned with the need to reassess liberal education, invited colleges to submit proposals for reexamining their objectives and for analyzing the relevance and adequacy of teaching techniques and other practices in relation to them. Between 1952 and 1954 the Fund made self-study grants to thirty-eight colleges (Donaldson, 1959). It is clear from Donaldson's report that the value of a self-study for the institution depends to a considerable degree on the quality of faculty and administrative participation in the self-study process. Whether or not recommendations for change will be put into effect is also greatly influenced by the presence or absence of a follow-up mechanism.

A follow-up of the recommendations emanating from a very extensive self-study at Syracuse University (Pace and Troyer, 1949) was unusual in many respects, and it has heretofore been reported only in the Ph.D. dissertation for which it was undertaken (Browne, 1952). Browne was basically trying to answer a question posed by the chancellor three years after the completion of the self-study: "Do we really know how much action has been taken with respect to all those recommendations that were made by the self-survey committees?" To provide the answer, Browne undertook the following analyses: A careful reading of the self-survey documents led him to identify some 500 separate recommendations, defined as calls for action of some sort. Then he classified each recommendation in six ways, according to (1) its area or topic (such as administrative organization, curriculum and instruction, finance, library, or plant facilities); (2) what type of action it called for (organizing, appointing, or shifting personnel; rendering a service; establishing or modifying a procedure; providing, changing, or withdrawing a facility; or rendering financial assistance; (3) how much action had been taken (full, partial, or no action); (4) the probable cost of acting on it (major, minor, or no cost); (5) its intended beneficiary (the administration, faculty, students, nonacademic personnel, specific instructional units, personnel units, business units, or the university as a whole); and (6) the level of responsibility for action or decision. For example, was it a recommendation that, if implemented, would need to go to the board of trustees? Or could it be implemented by the top management, by the senior administrators, by departmental or subunit heads, by faculty committees, or some other group?

By cross-tabulating the results of these classifications, Browne was able to answer such questions as the following: What subsequently happened to recommendations related to curriculum and instruction which involved no cost and which could be implemented at the faculty or departmental level? What happened to recommendations with respect to providing a facility, involving major cost, which would have to be authorized at the level of the board of trustees? Since the majority membership on all survey committees consisted of faculty members, did this result in a predominance of recommendations in which the faculty was the intended beneficiary? (The answer to that question was no.) In short, the follow-up study produced a diagnostic analysis of the impact of the self-study on changes at the university. Although the specific results of this analysis are only of historical interest, and primarily so to Syracuse, it is nevertheless worth noting that 65 percent of the self-study recommendations had been either fully or partially acted upon within three years following the publication of the self-study report. Incidentally, of course, the follow-up itself prompted action on some of the recommendations which had received no action up to that point. The manner in which recommendations were classified and analyzed could well serve as a model for studying the dynamics of change within an institution.

My impression is that special or ad hoc comprehensive self-studies involving extensive and intensive participation by the faculty and administration of an institution are less common today than they may have been a decade or two ago. Probably one reason for this reduction is that the value of a periodic review of purposes and programs has been rather thoroughly accepted and that most institutions have faculty committees or institutional research offices which provide continuing appraisal. Another reason, perhaps, is that a self-study is now a built-in requirement of accreditation review, and thus the process of self-study has been merged with the process of accreditation.

The Evolution of Accreditation Self-Studies. The need for minimum standards and definitions prompted the earliest forms of what we now call accreditation. In 1913, for example, eligibility for membership in the North Central Association was based on the following considerations: the institution had to offer a four-year curriculum, with 120 semester hours required for graduation; 15 units of high school work were required for admission; faculty training, salaries, and workload had to achieve a minimum level of acceptability; expenditures for library and laboratories had to meet a minimum figure; a specified minimum amount of money in endowments and in income was required; and finally, the institution had to offer a program of studies related to its resources.

Subsequently, the concept of standards came to be viewed as too rigid and restrictive because it might prevent innovation and experimentation. In 1929 the North Central Association established a Committee on the Revision of Standards. That group engaged in a very intensive survey of fifty-seven colleges and universities located in the north central area. The result of those surveys was the publication, in 1936, of a series of seven volumes under the general heading of *The Evaluation of Higher Institutions*. The first of those volumes, called *Principles of Accrediting Higher Institutions* (Zook and Haggerty, 1936), illustrates the new concepts and procedures that were advocated. The new statement of policy was described as follows (p. 98): "An institution will be judged for accreditment upon the basis of the total pattern it presents as an institution of higher education. While institutions will be judged in terms of each of the characteristics noted in this statement of policy, it is recognized that wide variations will appear in the degree of conformity realized. It is accepted as a principle of procedure that superiority in some characteristic may be regarded as compensating to some extent for deficiencies in other respects. The facilities and activities of an institution will be judged in terms of the purposes it seeks to serve." The word *standards* was eliminated in favor of *characteristics*. Thus the institution was to be viewed in relation to an extended list of characteristics. These were described as constituting an institutional pattern map, or an institutional profile.

The items to be considered included such matters as faculty, curriculum, instruction, library, student personnel service, administration, finance, and physical plant, with many subheadings included under each of these main areas. The quality or adequacy of the institution with respect to each characteristic was rated on a scale from 1 to 100, and a profile of institutional characteristics could then be drawn. The ratings were made by a team of observers from the regional association. The items to be rated were ones which had previously been found, in the extensive surveys of the fifty-seven institutions in the north central area, to have a positive relationship to judgments of institutional quality. This approach to accreditation had the advantage of specifying much more clearly the aspects of institutional functioning that should be observed, but it had the disadvantage of relying very heavily on the judgments of the observers.

Accreditation today does not follow such a detailed set of specifications. Rather, from an initial and fairly simple definition of standards and then from an overemphasis on a long list of specific characteristics, accreditation has moved toward a much greater emphasis on the self-study conducted by the institution before the visit of an accreditation team. All the regional accrediting associations now expect and require a self-study report as the first step in the accreditation process. Most of them have also produced manuals or handbooks describing some of the major elements that should be included in such a self-study. In addition, most self-study handbooks today stress the importance of assembling evidence with respect to students' learning and other indications of the success with which institutional objectives are being attained, although they retain in addition the former emphasis on institutional processes and characteristics. So contemporary self-studies involve a thorough consideration of institutional purposes, programs, operations, and results.

In the *Handbook for Institutional Self-Study* published by the Commission on Higher Education of the Middle States Association of Colleges and Schools (1978), a comprehensive self-study is described as encompassing the following major topics: goals and objectives, outcomes (educational effectiveness), program (instructional and noninstructional activities), students and student life, faculty, teaching, instructional resources and equipment, organization and governance, and financial planning. Relevant information needs to be assembled, analyzed, and discussed. Faculty members, administrators, trustees, and students are to participate in this activity. The result is an integrated portrait of the current status of the institution, its effectiveness, its need for change or improvement.

The best statement about the nature of a comprehensive self-study is Paul Dressel's chapter "Institutional Self-Study" in his recent book entitled *Handbook of Academic Evaluation* (1976). In fact, Dressel's book is the most thorough and comprehensive treatment of that broad topic that has yet been written.

Typically, the regional accrediting associations operate on a five-year cycle. Thus, every five years, more or less, institutions throughout the country engage in internal reviews of their activities and, in turn, are viewed externally by groups of their peers from other institutions representing the accrediting associations.

New Directions for Self-Studies. Although I regard the connection between self-studies and accreditation reviews as basically desirable because it encourages self-analysis, the value of self-study for the institution does not depend on that connection. It would no doubt be desirable to assess periodically the performance of a government bureau or program whether or not such assessment was required by an act of Congress or by an executive order. The value of self-study is inherent in the act itself. The value ultimately depends on the quality of the effort that goes into it, the dimensions that are explored, the methods and instruments for gathering data, and the perspective from which the activity is viewed.

Rather than thinking of self-study as a periodic activity, one should think of it as a developmental and cumulative activity. Given this point of view, it might be better to give it a new name. An important new direction for self-study and institutional research is what I choose to call institutional case studies. In a sense, one can regard case studies and comparative studies as complementary, but the difference between them is significant. An analogy with psychology may help to explain the significance. In psychology one can find two major traditions: the study of psychological phenomena and the study of lives. Major psychological phenomena are sensation, perception, learning, motivation, and so on. Through laboratory, comparative, and statistical studies, one measures individual differences and tries to explain how the phenomena operate, as well as to establish and predict relationships and consequences. The other tradition—the study of lives—focuses on the individual. It is clinical, developmental, sequential, and cumulative rather than experimental, comparative, or statistical. Each tradition produces valuable knowledge about human behavior; but each produces, at least to some extent, a different type of knowledge, a different sort of insight, and serves a somewhat different purpose. So too, in higher education, comparative knowledge about institutions in general and clinical knowledge about a single institution serve different purposes and produce different insights.

One might suppose that the institutional research office within the college would be the natural locus for ongoing institutional case study. But it might not be. Most such offices are beset by deadlines and heavily involved in basic accounting activities related to budget making, cost analysis, and similar matters, all of which orient the staff and its activities to serve administration and management. A knowledge of computers and data systems is often the main consideration in selecting a director of institutional research. The desirable talents for carrying on an institutional case study are quite different. Such talents would include a historical and philosophical view of the institution and of higher education in general; a knowledge and an understanding of curriculum and teaching and of student development and learning; sensitivity to the particular ambience of the institution and how that relates to its selective attraction for students, patrons, and others on whom its viability rests; the ability to identify and describe the dynamics of change—the people, the politics, the internal and external forces; the institutional mechanisms for responding to new circumstances; and the ability to select and collect information about the institution's effectiveness in fulfilling its diverse purposes. A case study cannot be a production-line activity, amassing data and assembling reports to meet a time schedule. A case study needs data, in large amounts, but it also requires time for exploration, for reflection, and for thoughtful evaluation. Some institutional research offices have the capacity for educational evaluation as well as institutional accounting. Some do not.

Ideally, institutional accounting and educational research and evaluations are complementary. Evaluation and research need the objective information base that comes from accurate enumeration and accounting. Accounting and cost analyses need the interpretive judgment that comes from research and evaluation. A college self-study is the natural occasion for merging these resources and lines of inquiry. The accumulation of self-studies constitutes a case history of the institution, or, as I prefer to call it, an institutional case study.

Beyond providing the current-status sort of information about the college, a case study should seek to understand the *dynamics* of institutional effectiveness and change. For this purpose, I have two models to suggest. The first is a model for studying students' learning and development and how the student and the institution interact in contributing to educational effectiveness. The second is a model for examining the dynamics of institutional change and adaptiveness to new circumstances.

The basic local question for evaluating students' development is quite simple: given the students who come here, what happens to them and what are they like when they leave? Answering this question obviously requires two measurements: before and after, at entrance and exit. Understanding development requires a knowledge of the intervening experiences and events that are intended to facilitate it. I think of this as a contextual model for evaluating student development and college impress. Note that I use the word *impress* rather than *impact*. Dictionary synonyms for *impact* include such words as *strike, force, blow, collision*. It does not strike me as an apt term for describing the effects of college on student development. Dictionary synonyms for the word *impress* include mark, stamp, characteristic, impression. I think college does mean to make a mark or impression on students.

The model has three basic propositions (see Figure 1). First, the college experience consists of the events one encounters in college. Second, the nature or meaning of these events, experiences, and encounters is influenced by certain features of the environment and by the amount, breadth, and quality of the effort students exert. And third, the combined influences of environment and effort lead to student development and college impress.

1. *Entrance.* Students coming into the college vary in prior experience, background, knowledge, personal traits, and so on. What one needs to know at this stage is their standing on a set of

Firgure 1. Path for a Student Development and College Impress Model

Entrance

Criterion measures at entrance

Knowledge
Critical thinking
Other skills
Interests
Values
Personal traits
and so on

College Experiences and Events

Salient facilities and opportunities

Classrooms
Library
Laboratories
Residence units
Student Union
Cultural facilities
Athletic and recreational facilities

Clubs and organizations
Student acquaintances
Faculty contacts
Experience in writing
Self-understanding

Effort and Environment

Amount, scope and quality of effort students invest in using the facilities and opportunities

Press of the college environment

Academic-scholarly emphasis
Esthetic-expressive emphasis
Critical-evaluative emphasis
Vocational emphasis

Nature of relationships in the college environment

With peers
With faculty members
With administrative offices

Exit

Student development and college impress as indicated by

Differences between criterion scores at entrance and exit

Self-ratings of progress, benefits, satisfactions

Attitudes toward the college

And, subsequently, evidence from alumni studies of continued interests, continued learning, and so on relevant criterion measures. Many personal traits and background factors are not criterion measures or outcome measures—such as age, sex, race, family income, high school grades, SAT scores, liberal-conservative attitudes, and introversion-extroversion. Measures of attitudes and personal traits are not appropriate as criterion or outcomes measures unless it is a purpose of the college to change these qualities—to make extroverts into introverts, conservatives into liberals, or vice versa. Moreover, traits that psychologists regard as relatively stable are not appropriate criteria when one's purpose is to measure change. Criterion or outcome measures define what the college hopes its students will be like when they finish. What knowledge, what understanding of important concepts and ideas, what critical-thinking and other skills, what interests or values should students possess when they graduate? In relation to these relevant criteria, where do students begin their college experience?

2. *College events and experiences.* Experience consists of events. The college experience consists of the events that occur in the college environment. Many of the salient events and experiences are clustered in a number of fairly common settings—classrooms, libraries, laboratories, residence units, athletic spaces, student unions, and places where cultural events such as art exhibits, concerts, and plays occur. Other events, having a less clearly defined physical location, consist of opportunities for associations and experiences that are available in the college setting—opportunities to have contacts with faculty members, to participate in clubs and organizations, to broaden and deepen one's acquaintances with other students, to improve one's writing skills, to grow in self-understanding. All these may be thought of as facilities, conditions, or opportunities provided by the college and intended to promote students' learning and development.

3. *Effort.* All learning and development requires an investment of time and effort by the student. What students can gain from the variety of events depends on the amount, scope, and quality of their engagement. As these encounters broaden and deepen, the student's capacity for growth is enhanced. To document objectively the scope and quality of students' effort is crucial for understanding growth and development. It is astonishing but true that almost no evaluations of higher education have considered, sys-

tematically and diagnostically, the role of student effort in the attainment of desired outcomes. What is the quality of the effort students invest in classroom learning? The range could be from relatively simple cognitive activities, such as taking notes and underlining, to higher-level cognitive activities, such as efforts to explain, organize, and go beyond assignments. What is the quality of the effort students make in using the library resources? Here the range might be from routine and moderately exploratory use, such as reading an assigned article or using the card catalog, to greater degrees of independent exploration and focused activity. What is the quality of students' efforts in making contact with faculty members? Those efforts could be mainly routine; or they could involve serious discussions about careers, seeking criticism of one's work, seeking personal counsel. With respect to all the salient facilities and opportunities the college has to offer, one can measure the quality of the effort students invest in using them.

4. *Environment*. The institution is an environment. The facilities it provides, the expectations it communicates, the behavior it rewards, the way its members relate to one another, and its policies, procedures, and programs create an atmosphere intended to exemplify its purposes. To the extent that this image or ethos is clearly perceived, it is a shaping force or stimulus for student development. With respect to the major goals of this environment—such as scholarship, critical-mindedness, esthetic awareness, and vocational development—the emphases range along a scale from strong to weak. With respect to the nature of interpersonal relationships, the environment can be placed on a scale ranging from friendly, congenial, and supportive to cool, distant, and impersonal. These environmental characteristics make up the institutional context and the stimulus for the amount, scope, and quality of students' effort.

5. *Exit*. When students leave college, the readministration of criterion measures applied when they entered provides the basic data for assessing the amount and direction of their learning and development. Additional measures related to changes in students' knowledge of their major field would also be relevant, taken first at the beginning of the junior year and later at the end of the senior year.

6. *Development and Impress*. Development is inferred from

the difference in scores at two points. Impress, in the sense of making an impression or leaving a mark on the student, is similarly inferred from differences in before and after scores on relevant criterion measures; but one can also regard impress as a personal feeling or belief on the part of the student. Thus, impress could be inferred from self-reports of change and progress toward desired goals, the benefits attributed to events and experiences, and expressions of satisfaction with college. Impress further implies a more lasting mark and hence could also be measured after college by indications of continued interests, outlooks, concerns, and so on, related to intellectual, cultural, personal, social, occupational, and other criteria.

Much of the needed instrumentation for this model of student development and college impress is now or may soon be available. The Area Tests of ETS's Undergraduate Assessment Program, designed for seniors, can be given to freshmen, too. The Field Tests of the Undergraduate Assessment Program, measuring students' knowledge of the major field, can also be given at two points. The newer measures being developed at ETS—measures of analytic thinking, synthesizing ability, communication, and awareness—are obviously relevant as well, as are the tests being developed in the College Outcome Measures Project at ACT.

In my own recent research activities I have constructed a set of measures of the quality of student effort. They have been pretested. They are simple, reliable, and valid. These measures were used experimentally in thirteen colleges and universities in the spring of 1979 and they are now available for use by any institution that wishes to have an inventory of the campus experiences and quality of effort of its students. The measures are part of a questionnaire called *College Student Experiences* (Pace, 1979). In format they are checklists of activities; students are asked to indicate about how often they have done each of them during the current school year by checking "never," "occasionally," "often," or "very often." The activities reflect different levels of quality of effort. Each facility and type of opportunity in the model described earlier is covered in the questionnaire. Since the focus of these measures is on learning and development, the selection of content within each scale was guided by basic concepts of learning and of development. In constructing some scales my colleagues and I were guided by concepts of learning that hold that some kinds of learning activity are at a higher cognitive level than others. Other scales were based on concepts of personality development. Personality develops as it encounters new experiences that require new modes of response. One does not grow without having something to grow on—some challenge, problem, or condition that stimulates new responses and perhaps new insight. There must, in other words, be some contact, some encounter, some set of events and experiences which, theoretically, reflect increasing levels of involvement, challenge, and effort. In the very broadest sense we had, in the back of our minds, the concept of capitalizing on the potential for learning and development inherent in the nature of a particular facility or a particular category of experience. A high score on a scale can only be obtained by engaging with some frequency in the higher-quality activities.

The complete questionnaire also elicits other pertinent information related to the model: the usual sort of background information about the respondents—such as age, sex, year in college, residence, racial or ethnic identification, parents' education, major field, part-time job, if any, and so on; a brief section measuring satisfaction with college; eight rating scales about aspects of the college environment; and students' ratings of how much gain or progress they feel they have made toward a list of eighteen objectives or outcomes. Thus, the questionnaire responses enable one to analyze the relationships among personal characteristics, college experiences, college environment, quality of effort, and progress toward important outcomes.

If one wished to characterize the overall environment in fuller detail than is provided by the rating scales in the College Student Experiences questionnaire, one could use the College and University Environment Scales (CUES). The CUES, discussed at length later in this section, is especially suited for use by liberal arts colleges. For universities or other more comprehensive environments, however, a more diagnostic measure would be more useful, simply because any large university has important subenvironments that may have a greater effect on students' behavior than does the overall or total environment. During the past dozen or so years Rudolph Moos and his colleagues at the Social Ecology Laboratory in Stanford, California (Moos, 1979), have studied a variety of educational environments, focusing on relatively small and readily comprehensible environments—college residence units, high school classrooms, hospital wards. Regardless of the particular environment, there consistently emerged three types of environmental characteristics: the characteristics related to its purposes, its human relationships, and its administration or management.

A few years ago I developed and used at UCLA a new environment questionnaire based on the dimensions suggested by Moos. There are, for example, four sets of items related to educational purposes of the institution—an academic-scholarly emphasis, an esthetic-expressive emphasis, a critical-evaluative emphasis, and a vocational emphasis. Other sets of items are related to human relationships within the environment, such as that between students and administrators. Each of these item sets forms a scale consisting of nine items. The scales related to educational purposes are to be answered with respect to the student's major field, thus enabling one to see whether the environmental press felt by humanities majors, for example, is different from the environmental press felt by physical science majors, or engineers, or other groups. The relationship scales—having to do with peers, faculty members, and administrators—are to be answered from the range of one's own experience rather than with regard to students in general, or the faculty in general. At the end of the questionnaire are a number of statements about the university as a whole. With a few minor changes this new environment questionnaire could be made available for use by any college or university.

As for instruments related to other parts of the model, one should consider at least some entrance and exit measures of attitudes, interests, and values that may be of particular relevance to the local institution, but I have no specific recommendations. And for analyzing longer-lasting impress, such as might be revealed by studies of alumni, the new directions I suggested at the end of the section on achievement after college would provide good instrumentation.

I have discussed this model of student development and college impress as one line of thinking about an institutional case study. Its local utility and value does not depend on comparing one's own institution with some other group of institutions. Its local value depends on the relevance of the information to local purposes. Of course, to the extent that case studies collect similar information, the accumulation of case studies would permit comparative analyses. But the virtue of thinking from a case-study perspective lies in the encouragement it may give to enrich objective data with local history, local purposes, special interests and aspirations, and on-campus discussions in a way that is not possible, or at least has not been tried, in national comparative studies. Finally, it should be noted that the developmental model I have described, by including effort and environment as major variables, reflects a reciprocal view of accountability. The institution is accountable for the facilities and the array of events it provides and for the environmental context in which they are embedded; the students are accountable for the amount, scope, and quality of the effort they invest in using the facilities and opportunities that are provided.

Another suggestion for the future study of institutions grows from the need to understand more fully the dynamics of institutional change and adaptiveness. Just as I have suggested, as one aspect of institutional case study, a developmental and dynamic model of students' progress through the college years, so I also suggest, as another aspect of institutional case study, a developmental and dynamic model of the institution as an organization, and specifically how it becomes aware of and adapts to changing circumstances. Accreditation and self-study have typically included a look at changing institutional goals and objectives and at the internal governance and administration. I am not addressing a new problem here, only presenting a way of thinking about it.

Some critics claim that colleges and universities are basically resistant to change. True, colleges are inherently conservative; they are conserving institutions, for that is one of their purposes. But they are also adaptive institutions. The judgment that they always resist change, responding only to the most enormous pressure on them, is a false judgment. It is a judgment that stems from a limited historical perspective and from the typical frustrations of reformers who discover that not everyone is immediately persuaded and prepared to do what they think should be done.

Major changes in any institution—whether in business, government, education, or the church—are primarily the result of forces outside the particular institution. Wars, depressions, population shifts, and other significant events in the larger society induce changes in the organization and activity of government. Inventions, technology, natural resources, and life styles induce changes in production, distribution, services, and other activities of business and industry. So, too, the relevance of knowledge, understanding, and expertise for an increasingly broad spectrum of society has induced major changes in colleges and universities.

The modern university has little or no resemblance to the colonial colleges of the seventeenth century or to the colleges of the eighteenth century—in clientele, curriculum, or methods of teaching. Science, empirical inquiry, modern languages and literature, the social sciences, academic departments, credit hours, distribution requirements, training for various occupations, women students, adult education—none of these can be found in the colonial colleges. Also unknown in the colonial colleges were such teaching methods as lectures, discussions, seminars, laboratories, field trips, and audiovisual presentations. The rise of the modern university from the latter part of the nineteenth century to the early part of the twentieth century has been well described by historian Laurence Veysey (1965). And the changes in curriculum from colonial days to the present have been charted by historian Frederick Rudolph (1977). In any one period, especially to the reformers of the day, the struggle to bring about change is always seen as painfully slow, as facing difficult odds and entrenched interests. It took several decades, for instance, to get science and modern languages into the curriculum. But viewed from a greater distance, the changes in higher education from colonial Harvard to contemporary Michigan represent a total transformation. From that perspective, colleges and universities emerge as highly adaptive organizations.

David Henry (1975, p. 148), looking back over the four decades from the 1930s to the 1970s, observed that "three elements stand out: the oscillations in growth and their consequences; the constancy of change; the significance of public evaluation and the nature of public interaction." Note especially Henry's observation that even within the limited time of four decades, one element that stands out is the constancy of change. And even though there have surely been periods of relative inaction, any view of higher education which encompasses several decades or several centuries would lead us to agree with Clark Kerr's assessment that "higher education in the U.S. has a remarkable record of constructive adaptation to changing circumstances" (quoted in Henry, p. 147).

What are some of the major adaptations that colleges and universities have made in the past forty or fifty years? They adjusted to the Great Depression in the 1930s, when resources were severely limited and faculty salaries declined. They adapted to World War II, when enrollments dropped about 20 percent and a variety of war-related services were undertaken. And after that shrinkage they nevertheless handled the sudden surge of enrollments with the return of the veterans. They responded to Sputnik by incorporating large-scale research activities, often in special institutes. Then they adapted to another burst of enrollments—from about two and a half million in 1950 to more than ten million in 1977—an adaptation not accompanied by a correspondingly large rise in financial resources. Meanwhile they dealt with the campus turbulence of the 1960s over civil rights and Vietnam.

Perhaps one of the differences between the present and earlier times is the speed with which external events have an impact on the organization. It is a difference that more than ever suggests the need for alert adaptive mechanisms within the organization and that gives particular relevance to understanding the dynamics of institutional change.

For the model presented next I am indebted to one of my former doctoral students, Terrence Feuerborn (1971), whose dissertation examined the literature on organizational change in industry, in sociological theory, and in education, and developed a synthesis of concepts which he regarded as especially useful for higher education.

The first feature of the model (Figure 2) is labeled the Task Environment. This consists of events occurring outside the institution that may bear on the institution's tasks—its mission, programs, and activities. I have just noted some of the events and forces during the past four decades. At the present time the task environment would surely include the lower birthrate, inflation, the job market for college graduates, the competition for public funds, and many other conditions.

The second element in the model, called Awareness, is con-

Figure 2. Model for Analyzing the Dynamics of Institutional Change

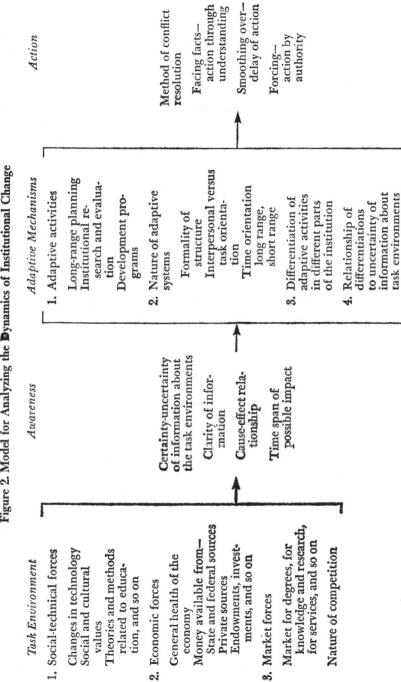

Task Environment

1. Social-technical forces

   Changes in technology
   Social and cultural values
   Theories and methods related to education, and so on

2. Economic forces

   General health of the economy
   Money available from—
   State and federal sources
   Private sources
   Endowments, investments, and so on

3. Market forces

   Market for degrees, for knowledge and research, for services, and so on

   Nature of competition

Awareness

Certainty-uncertainty of information about the task environments

Clarity of information

Cause-effect relationship

Time span of possible impact

Adaptive Mechanisms

1. Adaptive activities

   Long-range planning
   Institutional research and evaluation
   Development programs

2. Nature of adaptive systems

   Formality of structure
   Interpersonal versus task orientation
   Time orientation long range, short range

3. Differentiation of adaptive activities in different parts of the institution

4. Relationship of differentiations to uncertainty of information about task environments

Action

Method of conflict resolution

Facing facts—action through understanding

Smoothing over—delay of action

Forcing—action by authority

cerned with how information about the task environment does or does not enter the organization and how its members respond to that information. The institution may be so insulated that it is unaware of what is happening out there. The information may be conflicting. People may not be sure that these external forces will have an effect, or, if they do, that the effect will apply to their institution. People may also be uncertain about how soon an impact will be felt. Or they may simply disbelieve. In the American automobile industry disbelief in the demand for small cars with better fuel economy and less pollution was widespread a decade ago. But events in the task environment from Germany, Japan, OPEC, and Washington, D.C., compelled change. In some colleges and universities, people know about the declining birthrate, and yet do not believe it will affect their own enrollments. They may be right. In any case these external events are perceived and interpreted with varying degrees of certainty.

The third element is called Adaptive Mechanisms, which indentifies and suggests ways of characterizing the subsystems of the organization that are related to its adaptiveness. Included are its mechanisms for long-range planning and development and for institutional research and evaluation. These subsystems operate with different degrees of formal structure, have various interpersonal orientations, and differ in their focus on short-range versus long-range matters. Then, because a university is a complex and diverse institution, adaptive mechanisms in different parts of the institution may deal with somewhat differentiated problems. The task environment of the Medical School or the School of Engineering differs in some ways from the task environment of the College of Arts and Sciences or from the adult education program in Extension. And finally, uncertainty about the task-environment information varies from one part of the institution to another. These are suggested ways of examining the adaptive mechanisms and how they function.

The result of all these activities generates conflict, owing to uncertainties, to differences in judgment, and to the varying implications the task environment has for different segments of the organization. The likelihood of change, and especially of constructive change, then comes down to methods of conflict resolution or taking action. One can set the problem aside, hoping it will go away. Maybe it will, or maybe the problem will appear later in a more aggravated form. Meanwhile the prestige and importance attached to the adaptive mechanism will be undermined. Or one can take action by administrative order. The action may have merit but may not be understood by the faculty and others in the organization. This can undermine morale. Or, best of all, one can face the facts fairly, confront the evidence openly, and agree on a course of action—an agreement based on shared knowledge and understanding.

An institutional case study needs to examine how the organization adapts to changing circumstances. This model may be useful in guiding that examination.

Comparative and Interinstitutional Studies

Before the 1930s many surveys of higher education were made, varying considerably in quality as well as scope. There were national surveys, state and regional surveys, surveys of particular types or groups of institutions, and surveys of single institutions. The main topics of inquiry included the organization, the staff, finances, the plant, students, curriculum and instruction, and special services. The popularity of surveys, no doubt in part a reflection of the rapidly emerging prestige of science, objectivity, and fact finding as a significant base for understanding institutions and enlightened policy, led the president of the Carnegie Foundation for the Advancement of Teaching to invite Walter Crosby Eells, of Stanford University, to make a critical analysis of the surveys, to appraise their value and utility, and to consider standards for their improvement in the future and their significance in developing a science of higher education.

Eells (1937) identified 230 printed survey reports, as well as 348 other survey reports available only in typed or mimeographed form. The 230 printed reports were the main focus of Eells's analyses—61 national or regional surveys of higher education, 51 state surveys, 49 surveys of individual institutions, and 69 national, regional, state, and city surveys of education in which higher education was a special topic or section. The rise in the popularity of surveys is shown by the fact that of the 230 printed survey reports, 39 were published before 1919, 97 in the ten-year period from 1919 to 1928, and 94 in the six-year period from 1929 to 1934.

The motivations for making surveys, particularly in the twenties and thirties, will seem familiar to many contemporary readers: the rapid growth of enrollments in higher education; the increased complexity of the system, suggesting the need for coordination and state planning; the growing size and complexity of universities; the increased costs and the demands on state budgets for the public institutions and corresponding problems for private colleges; a concern for greater efficiency—in short, the need for systematic information about a fast-growing, increasingly complex and costly enterprise.

From the number and scope of surveys in the first third of the twentieth century, one can infer that little systematic, objective, and comparative information about colleges and universities had been assembled before then. One can also infer that many people in higher education believed that such information was important and useful. Much of what was collected in these early surveys was what we would today consider basic census-type data; namely, an enumeration and description of current conditions and practices. If much of it now seems elementary and familiar, one must remember that in those days it was unfamiliar and highly revealing about the status of higher education.

One of the studies briefly mentioned in Eells's review was a survey of 35 colleges related to the Methodist Episcopal Church (Reeves and others, 1932). This survey illustrates the scope and detail of the information that was characteristically included in the best of these early surveys. Among the fifty or more different topics studied in the Methodist college survey, here are a few examples: enrollment trends, student retention, charters and bylaws, physical plant facilities and conditions, course offerings and degrees, class size and faculty load, salaries, retirement provisions, student counseling, budgetary procedures, income and indebtedness, tuition and fees, educational costs. As a result of these surveys, the various colleges affiliated with the Methodist church were able to see the extent to which they differed from others and to consider the adequacy of their own conditions and practices. Moreover, the survey team consisted of experts who had conducted many other surveys and had looked in detail at many other institutions, not only by means of visits to the campus but through interviews with administrators and others, the detailed examination of records and reports, and the administration of common questionnaires and other data-gathering devices; these people were therefore in a position to make judgments about the arrangements and practices they felt were desirable. In other words, surveys characteristically resulted in a set of recommendations for the improvement of institutional conditions and practices.

Eells's report presents some evidence of the extent to which various recommendations growing out of the early education surveys were implemented. In a group of 50 separate surveys, which altogether involved 189 institutions, a total of nearly 5,000 specific recommendations were identified. The chief administrative officer, usually the college president at the institution studied, was given a list of the survey recommendations that had been made and was asked to indicate what had subsequently happened with respect to those recommendations. Their responses indicated that within a period of three years, 37 percent of the recommendations had been carried out fully, and an additional 8 percent had been carried out sometime after three years; thus a total of 45 percent of the recommendations were carried out in full. Recommendations partially carried out accounted for 20 percent within three years and an additional 6 percent subsequently, leaving 29 percent that were described as not carried out at all. Clearly, much of what was done in these surveys resulted in recommendations that found a receptive audience and that were subsequently put into practice.

In many respects, the impact of these surveys was both profound and pervasive. For example, the survey of medical education in the United States and Canada (Flexner, 1910) resulted in the closing of dozens of medical schools owing to the evidence presented on their inadequacies of financing, clinical facilities, curriculum, standards for admission, and standards for graduation. Moreover, the Flexner report was very instrumental in upgrading the standards of those medical schools that survived his clinical, objective dissection. Similar surveys resulting in improved standards were made of engineering education, of legal education, of dental education, and of other professional schools. The federal government, through its Bureau of Education, surveyed Negro schools and colleges and land-grant colleges and assisted in several statewide surveys. Indeed, the

U.S. Bureau of Education appointed a specialist in higher education, and among the activities of that higher education component of the Bureau was the initiation of surveys. Today, of course, the Office of Education and other parts of the Department of Health, Education, and Welfare routinely carry out statistical studies of colleges and universities. Another result of these early surveys, particularly their revelation of chaotic conditions with respect to faculty retirement policies, led the Carnegie Foundation for the Advancement of Teaching to create the Teachers' Insurance Annuity Association, which today everyone knows as TIAA. In short, these early surveys did have a considerable impact.

The surveys were more than just descriptive. They were also, in some respects, analytical. In order to make comparisons among institutions, the researchers had to devise common definitions of the data elements to be collected. What, for example, is a full-time student or full-time faculty member? How does one calculate the student-faculty ratio? How does one develop an index of instructional cost per student credit hour? How does one compare faculty salaries when in some cases they are for nine months' work and in other cases for ten or eleven months'? And who, indeed, are faculty members? Are part-time instructors included? If so, how does one combine the information in order to make statements about average faculty salaries? These and many other matters had to be resolved in order to make surveys comparative.

The need for common definitions was recognized very early. As early as the 1930s there was a national committee on standard reports for institutions of higher education. In the 1950s, the American Council on Education established a special commission to consider the definition problem, and it made a variety of recommendations. In the 1960s and 1970s, a major activity of the National Center for Higher Education Management Systems has been the effort to develop standard definitions for such old but refractory concepts as a full-time student, a full-time faculty member, the classification of subjects and curricula, and the computation of instructional costs. Whether the problem will ever be solved to the satisfaction of those who think that everyone ought to do the same thing is perhaps questionable; whether it really needs to be solved is debatable, too. Of course, when one is comparing some particular subset of reasonably comparable institutions, one must be able to describe them in similar terms. But whether one can compare Harvard, Columbia, the University of Michigan, and other such institutions, using comparable terms and definitions, with small denominational liberal arts colleges, or with community colleges, or with military schools, is a question that has not really been answered. There are, of course, hazards in common definitions simply because although they are "common" on paper, they do not necessarily have a common meaning in a particular institution. For example, a recent study in California showed that the cost of library facilities per student at UCLA was substantially higher than that at other institutions. Was that bad? On further inspection—and this meant individual, on-site inquiry—the examiner discovered that approximately a fourth to a third of the users of the UCLA library were not UCLA students; they were students from other institutions in southern California, faculty members in other institutions, and the general public. And that was why the library cost per student appeared to be unusually high. This is simply to say that one cannot, despite common definitions, assume that the results produced from them are comparable in meaning. Nevertheless, the impetus given to the periodic census of conditions and practices in colleges and universities by the national, state, and special surveys of the 1930s has continued to the present day. Of course it is important to have accurate census data about what is going on. Of course it is also important to look behind the census to identify the reasons for the differences that are revealed.

Skipping ahead and ignoring many hundreds of intervening surveys, one can easily identify another major landmark inquiry in the 1940s (President's Commission on Higher Education, 1947). The task of the Commission appointed by President Truman at the end of World War II was to define the responsibilities of colleges and universities in American democracy and, more specifically, to examine their objectives, methods, and facilities in light of the social role higher education should play. The steady increase in the number of young people seeking a college education was accompanied by questions about how well the resources, the equipment, and the curriculum were keeping pace with the enrollment and with the increasing diversity of those students' needs and interests. The Commission therefore examined in some detail the objectives of general education; the question of access to higher education—the barriers to educational opportunity, such as economic barriers, regional variations, racial and religious barriers, the problem of equalizing opportunity; and the problem of assessing the relevance of higher education for those who might profit from it. The Commission further examined the condition of various segments of higher education, such as the community colleges, the liberal arts colleges, the professional schools, and the graduate schools. The many data-gathering inquiries initiated by the Commission were to provide the factual base for judgments about existing inequalities and about existing and potential opportunities for greater service. Among the recommendations of the Commission was a substantial expansion of the community colleges. That, subsequently, has been achieved. Major progress has also been made in reducing the economic, racial, and religious barriers to higher education that had been identified by President Truman's Commission. Following another recommendation, the federal government has greatly increased its financial aid to students. Without detailing any further the many recommendations of the Commission, I can simply state that this particular survey was probably the most extensive *single* inquiry into the status of higher education that has been made in the twentieth century.

When we turn to the most extensive *collection* of scholarly inquiries, however, we will be looking at the work of the Carnegie Commission on Higher Education in the 1960s and '70s (Carnegie Commission, 1974, 1975). The work of the Carnegie Commission is eclectic. It brought into being inquiries related to the history of higher education, the curriculum, the philosophy and purposes of institutions, the relation between institutions and the state, the issue of the control and governance of institutions, the relation of higher education to the labor market, the production of Ph.D.s, the role of higher education in expanding access for minority groups, the economic and financial problems and difficulties of higher institutions, the condition of various segments of higher education—such as science, the arts, the denominational schools, the Catholic colleges, the state colleges, the small liberal arts colleges, the community colleges, the professional schools, and the research institutes—and many, many other problems and conditions characterizing higher education at this time. Although many of the Commission's inquiries were not surveys of the sort I have been describing, the work as a whole can be described as a survey and appraisal of American higher education. It is unquestionably the most impressive collection of scholarly literature about colleges and universities that has yet been assembled. I would be surprised if any comparable body of literature existed about any other major institution in Western society.

Surveys of higher education, as well as of individual institutions, have continued to be made at both the state and federal level. For example, most states have now developed master plans for higher education. The development of master plans requires initially a survey of the educational needs and resources within the state and a firm base of information from which to develop coordinated proposals for future development. The Academy for Educational Development, a private nonprofit research and consulting firm, has within the past fifteen years or so conducted surveys and developed master plans in approximately twenty states.

Another development, although it does not fall under the heading of comparative studies, is worth noting here. This was the encouragement, first by the Carnegie Corporation and later by the Fund for the Advancement of Education of the Ford Foundation, of management surveys, mainly in the 1950s. For example, the Carnegie Corporation made matching grants to Vanderbilt, Oberlin, Vassar, Syracuse, and Johns Hopkins for management surveys of those institutions, employing the management consulting firm of Cresap, McCormick, and Paget. Subsequently the Ford Foundation enabled many other colleges and universities to employ management consultants to examine their operations.

The regional education associations, such as the Southern Regional Education Board and the Western Interstate Commission for Higher Education, have also undertaken a continuing program of surveys of higher education institutions within their regions. At the national level, the National Center for Educational Statistics annually collects information from all higher institutions with respect to students, programs, enrollment, degrees, and many other items under the general heading of the Higher Education General Information Survey (HEGIS). Over the years this data base has continued to grow, both in size and in sophistication. Few long-range plans or projections are possible without the existence of such a data base.

Comparative Studies of Institutional Goals. Within the past ten to fifteen years there have been several new lines of inquiry into the characteristics of colleges and universities as organizations—their structure and governance, their environment or atmosphere, and their internal functioning. From these inquiries it is possible to document some connections among organizational goals, organizational characteristics, and organizational achievement or output.

Scholars who write about colleges and universities as organizations have offered various models for describing them. That is not surprising, because in many respects colleges and universities are unique organizations. They are not entrepreneurial organizations producing a product for profit. They are not like classic bureaucratic organizations, such as the military or government agencies. They are not volunteer or service organizations. And they are not community or communal organizations, such as families or neighborhood groups. Indeed, in a study of college presidents (Cohen and March, 1974), the authors suggest that colleges belong to a class of organizations that can be labeled organized anarchies—characterized by problematic goals, unclear technology, and fluid participation. "The American college or university is a prototypic organized anarchy. It does not know what it is doing. Its goals are either vague or in dispute. Its technology is familiar but not understood. Its major participants wander in and out of the organization. These factors do not make a university a bad organization or a disorganized one; however, they do make it a problem to describe, understand, and lead" (p. 3).

It is true that colleges and universities have multiple goals and that some goals are clearer and more widely accepted than others. It is also true that faculty members have considerable autonomy and independence—much more than would be the case in a typical bureaucracy or a business organization. But even Cohen and March, in using the term *organized* anarchies, acknowledge that colleges and universities are indeed organizations. As they have become larger organizations, requiring increased amounts of state and federal support and subject to increased demands for accountability, they have grown to look more like bureaucracies, albeit loosely structured ones. A characteristic of organizations, in contrast with other forms of association, is that they have purposes. And as we shall see, despite Cohen and March's assertion, the major goals of colleges and universities are neither vague nor in serious dispute. Moreover, certain organizational characteristics are related to these major goals and to their achievement.

Three landmark questionnaires provide evidence on this topic. The first (Gross and Grambsch, 1974) is a survey of the organizational goals of universities, showing the extent to which there is agreement about goals and how the emphasis on certain goals is related to different sources of power within the universities. The second was based on the administration of the Institutional Goals Inventory at different types of institutions (Peterson and Uhl, 1977). The third consisted of administrations of the Institutional Functioning Inventory (Peterson and others, 1970).

Gross and Grambsch studied universities twice, first in 1964 and later in 1971. From the president, vice presidents, deans and directors, and selected department chairmen and faculty members at each of sixty-eight universities, responses were obtained to a list of forty-seven statements about university goals. Each statement of a goal was answered in two ways: How important is this aim at this university? And, How important should this aim be at this university? The response choices were "of absolutely top importance," "of great importance," "of medium importance," "of little importance," "of no importance." From each university approximately seventy people responded to the list of goal statements, all of whom presumably had a substantial amount of experience and observation on which to base their ratings. On the five-point rating scale the mean scores of all the responses from all the universities ranged from 3.90 to 2.41 with respect to the perceived importance of the goals and from 4.27 to 2.22 with respect to the preferred importance of the goals. Moreover, for both sets of ratings, the standard deviations were typically about .8, which indicates that the standard error of the means—that is, their stability—was about .2. What these results say is that there are indeed differences in the degree of importance attributed to various university goals and that there is considerable agreement or reliability with respect to these differences. When all the mean scores are arranged in order from highest to lowest, and when the orders of 1964 are compared with those of 1971, they are remarkably similar. In fact, for thirty-eight of the forty-seven goals, the two rankings of their perceived importance did not differ by more than four places in the order; and for forty of the forty-seven goals the rankings did not differ by more than five places. In short, knowledgeable reporters at these universities do know what the goals are, and they agreed about their relative importance both in 1964 and in 1971. Because their agreement both times is so high, I only report below the results of the most recent survey.

What, then, are the major goals about which there appears to be substantial agreement? The ten listed here are the ones that ranked among the top fifteen (out of forty-seven) with respect to both their *perceived* importance and their *preferred* importance.

1. Protect the faculty's right to academic freedom.
2. Maintain top quality in those programs we feel to be especially important (other programs, of course, being up to acceptable standards).
3. Increase the prestige of the university, or, if you believe it is already extremely high, ensure the maintenance of that prestige.
4. Train students in methods of scholarship and/or scientific research and/or creative endeavor.
5. Keep up to date and responsive.
6. Involve the faculty in the government of the university.
7. Maintain top quality in all programs we engage in.
8. Serve as a center for the dissemination of new ideas that will change the society, whether those ideas are in science, literature, the arts, or politics.
9. Protect and facilitate the students' right to inquire into, investigate, and examine critically any idea or program they might get interested in.
10. Produce a student who, whatever else may be done to him, has had his intellect cultivated to the maximum.

These are the major goals that characterize universities in general—that is, as a class of organization. But of course universities are not all alike. Some are private, some are public; some have a higher proportion of graduate students and award more doctorates than others; some are much more heavily engaged in research than others; and some have higher prestige or status than others. Related to these differences in institutional characteristics, there are clear differences in the relative importance of various goals. The goals that are most emphasized at private universities in general and at universities (public or private) with large graduate programs and a high volume of contract research are the following:

- Carry on pure research
- Encourage graduate work
- Maintain top quality in all programs
- Cultivate students' intellect
- Develop students' objectivity
- Train students in methods of scholarship and research
- Serve as a center for the preservation of the cultural heritage
- Admit only students of high potential
- Protect academic freedom
- Protect students' right of inquiry
- Increase or maintain prestige
- Maintain top quality in important programs
- Reward faculty for contribution to their profession or discipline

In contrast, the goals most emphasized at public universities in general and at universities (public or private) with small graduate programs and a low volume of contract research are distinctively different:

- Educate to the utmost high school graduates
- Assist citizens through extension programs
- Provide community cultural leadership
- Satisfy area needs
- Carry on applied research
- Provide special adult training
- Provide student activities
- Cultivate students' taste

- Ensure favor of validating bodies
- Emphasize undergraduate instruction
- Keep costs down

As organizations, then, these two kinds of universities are clearly different. The ones having fewer graduate students and doing less research accord greater importance to goals that reflect the land-grant traditions of applied research, service to the community, and relatively open admissions policies. The others stress goals that reflect the value of pure research, advanced scholarship, and the education of an elite constituency.

These different patterns of emphasis are further related to the power structures that influence the university's goals. To get at this relationship, Gross and Grambsch asked the respondents to indicate "how much say" they believed persons in various positions had in affecting the major goals of the university as a whole. Except for three of the power holders, the rank order of influence turned out to be almost identical in the public and the private universities. The three exceptions are legislators and state government (whose influence is much greater in the public institutions) and sources of grants (which have more influence in the private institutions). More revealing and diagnostic than these obviously expected differences, however, are the directions in which the scores of the two groups differ. For all the power holders that we can describe as internal— president, vice presidents, deans, department chairmen, faculty members, and students—the mean scores in the private universities are higher than the mean scores in the public universities. For nearly all the power holders that are external—trustees, legislators, state and federal government, citizens, and parents—the mean scores in the public universities are higher than the mean scores in the private universities. The influence of alumni is about the same in both types of institution. The only external power that is perceived as greater in private than in public universities is sources of grants and endowments.

Institutions whose goals are most affected by internal power emphasize such goals as cultivating students' intellect, affecting students with great ideas, training students for scholarship/research, accepting good students only, and protecting academic freedom.

These goals are deemphasized in institutions having a high external power structure, which stress different goals: preparing students for useful careers, assisting citizens through extension programs, providing community cultural leadership, and educating to the utmost high school graduates.

All the five goals emphasized by universities with high internal power and correspondingly deemphasized by universities with high external power are also goals that are significantly related to one or more of the indicators of research and scholarly productivity. If we regard research and scholarly productivity as a measure of institutional achievement, then such achievement is clearly connected with organizational characteristics—that is, with who has the most say about the importance of institutional goals.

The second major source of data about institutional goals comes from the use of the Institutional Goals Inventory (IGI) published by Educational Testing Service. The Inventory is similar to the one developed by Gross and Grambsch in several aspects. First, it asks respondents to rate each of the goals in two ways—how important the goal is at their institution and also how important they think it should be. Second, the ratings are arranged along a five-point scale, with the levels of importance ranging from "of no importance or not applicable," to "of extremely high importance." And third, many of the goal statements in the IGI are parallel in content (although not identical in wording) to those developed by Gross and Grambsch. The IGI, however, covers a broader range of goals because it is intended for a more diverse set of institutions—for two-year colleges, liberal arts colleges, and comprehensive universities offering less than the doctorate, as well as doctorate-granting universities. Of the ninety goal statements in the Inventory eighty are grouped into sets of four and scored in relation to each of twenty goal areas.

For reporting here I have selected the results obtained from extensive use of the IGI in California: results from 551 faculty members on eight campuses of the University of California; 1,394 faculty members from sixteen of the state universities and colleges; 3,938 faculty members from sixty-three community colleges; and 785 faculty members from eighteen private four-year colleges. When the mean ratings of importance given to each of the twenty goal

areas are computed and then arranged in rank order, the resulting
ranks for each of the four types of institutions reveal a number of
major differences.

For example, the eight campuses of the University of California have top goals very similar to those identified by Gross and
Grambsch. Research and advanced training were strongly emphasized goals among the highly research-oriented campuses. Freedom,
as measured by the IGI, includes academic freedom for the faculty
and also freedom of inquiry for the students. Both were among the
major goals of the research universities measured by Gross and

Table 19. Rank Order of Goals from Faculty Ratings in California Colleges

	University of California	California State Universities and Colleges	Community Colleges	Private 4-Year Colleges
Research	1	17	18	19
Advanced training	2	14	19	20
Freedom	3	3	6	4
Academic development	4	1	4	1
Accountability/ efficiency	5	2	5	6
Intellectual/esthetic environment	6	12	11	8
Intellectual orientation	7	7	12	5
Community	8	4	7	2
Innovation	9	13	10	7
Democratic government	10	6	9	9
Public service	11	15	15	17
Meeting local needs	12	9	2	13
Vocational preparation	13	5	1	14
Individual personal development	14	8	8	3
Cultural/esthetic awareness	15	10	14	11
Humanism/altruism	16	11	13	10
Social criticism/ activism	17	18	16	15
Social egalitarianism	18	16	3	16
Off-campus learning	19	19	17	18
Traditional religiousness	20	20	20	12

Source: Peterson, 1973, p. 164.

Grambsch. Academic development and intellectual orientation like-wise are similar to the Gross and Grambsch goals described as train-ing students in the methods of scholarship and research and produc-ing a student who has had his intellect cultivated to the maximum. The IGI goal called intellectual/esthetic environment does not have an exact parallel in the previous study, but it does refer to the intel-lectual vitality and excitement that characterizes the college environ-ment, along with an emphasis on a broad range of cultural activities. Except for the goal that IGI calls accountability/efficiency, a goal that everyone thinks is emphasized and that does not have a clear counterpart in the Gross and Grambsch study, the two surveys, using different statements and different populations, produce re-markably similar results.

The most important goals at the community colleges are vocational preparation, meeting local needs, and social egalitarian-ism. Social egalitarianism is defined as open admission and as the provision of the necessary remedial programs to serve those students who are admitted. This goal ranks near the bottom of the list at the University of California, a ranking consistent with the Gross and Grambsch survey, which showed that among the research-oriented universities, a major goal was to admit good students only.

Among the private four-year colleges, great importance is attached to the goal of facilitating the personal development of students and to generating a sense of community and loyalty and easy communication among administrators, faculty members, and students. These are surely goals that capitalize on the special char-acteristics of small private liberal arts colleges. All institutions attach high importance to the student's academic development.

To make the differences among the three kinds of institu-tions even clearer, we can look at their most distinguishing goals. Note in Table 20, for example, that for the University of California the goals of research, advanced training, freedom, and intellectual/esthetic environment differentiate the University of California from the other types of institutions. At the private four-year colleges the goals of individual personal development, community, intellectual orientation, humanism/altruism, and traditional religiousness are the ones that make them most different from the others. This finding is explained in part by the fact that about two-thirds of the private

Table 20. Illustrative Differences in Mean Scores of the Importance of
Goals from Faculty Ratings at Four Types of Institutions in California

	University of California	State Universities and Colleges	Community Colleges	Private 4-year Colleges
Goals emphasized by the University of California				
Research	3.82	3.43	1.57	2.13
Advanced training	3.50	2.57	1.55	2.04
Freedom	3.44	3.07	3.17	3.18
Intellectual/Esthetic environment	3.13	2.60	2.84	3.04
Goals emphasized by private 4-year colleges				
Individual personal development	2.62	2.65	3.03	3.26
Community	3.04	2.79	3.08	3.28
Intellectual orientation	3.08	2.75	2.86	3.10
Humanism/Altruism	2.57	2.59	2.76	3.06
Traditional religiousness	1.23	1.33	1.43	2.73
Goals emphasized by community colleges				
Vocational preparation	2.61	2.72	3.37	2.34
Meeting local needs	2.70	2.67	3.30	2.47
Social egalitarianism	2.35	2.47	3.20	2.33

Source: Peterson and Uhl, 1977, adapted from table 5.2, pp. 63–67.

four-year colleges included in this study had some connection with
a religious group, either Protestant or Catholic. That connection also
helps to explain the stress on the goal labeled humanism/altruism,
which is defined as a consciousness of moral issues and a concern
for the general welfare of humanity. The goals receiving greatest
emphasis in the community colleges have previously been noted.
Thus each type of institution has its own priorities, priorities that
fit its mission and that distinguish it from the other types.

The ratings reported above are based on faculty members'
perceptions of what is important at their institution. Although the
IGI was also used with administrators at half of these California
schools, I have not reported those results for the simple reason that
they are virtually the same as those from the faculties.

The ratings of what *should be* important compared with what *is* show that the *should be* ratings are almost always higher than the *is* ratings. This finding may simply reflect the desire of most people to be better than they are. What is interesting, however, is that despite the typical differences between the "perceived" and "preferred" ratings, all constituent groups are alike in their relative preferences. If faculty members think a goal should be more strongly emphasized than it is, so also do administrators and students. There is, in other words, no sharp conflict about goals among the three.

If there were any validity to Cohen and March's assertion that the goals of universities are either vague or in dispute, results such as those reported here would be impossible. The various segments of higher education—the universities, the state colleges, the community colleges, and the private four-year colleges—are indeed different from one another, and this differentiation in the relative importance of various goals is clearly evident. There are, moreover, specific organizational or institutional characteristics associated with different goal emphases. For example, the importance attributed to the goals of advanced training and research is positively correlated with the SAT scores of entering freshmen, the number of library books, income per student, the percentage of faculty members with doctoral degrees, and the number of graduate programs and graduate students. In contrast, when top importance is attributed to the goals of vocational preparation, meeting local needs, and social egalitarianism, the relationship of every one of the factors noted above is reversed, becoming negative. The goal of personal development is negatively related to the size of the institution (small is better) and negatively related to the percentage of faculty with doctorates, the number of graduate programs, and the number of graduate students. The goal of an intellectual/esthetic environment is positively related to the SAT scores of entering freshmen, the number of library books per student, income per student, and the percentage of freshmen choosing majors in liberal arts. So again we see that specific institutional characteristics are associated with different patterns of goal emphasis.

A somewhat different approach to the study of institutional purposes and practices is illustrated by the Institutional Functioning Inventory (IFI) (Peterson and others, 1970). The initial intent in constructing the IFI was to develop an objective measure of institutional practices and conditions that might be related to its readiness to accept new ideas, to be experimental and adaptive. The phrase *institutional vitality* was used to express this focus. In format, the Inventory consists of 132 statements. Some of these statements are answered by checking yes or no, others by checking agree or disagree. The statements themselves are grouped into eleven topics or aspects of institutional functioning, and 12 items compose the score on each topic. The scores, then, are based partly on knowledge of specific institutional events and practices and partly on opinions or perceptions of institutional policies and conditions. An example of a knowledge item is "Reports of various institutional studies are announced generally and made available to the entire teaching and administrative staff." An example of an opinion item is "Most administrators and faculty tend to see little real value in data-based institutional self-study." Those two items come from a scale labeled "Self Study and Planning." The IFI has been used in more than 150 colleges and universities; the responses to it have come primarily from samples of faculty members at those institutions, but also in many cases from administrators. Responses to some of the IFI scales have come from students as well.

The topics or aspects of institutional functioning measured by the questionnaire are as follows: Intellectual/Esthetic Extracurriculum, Freedom, Human Diversity, Concern for the Improvement of Society, Concern for Undergraduate Learning, Democratic Governance, Meeting Local Needs, Self-Study and Planning, Concern for Advancing Knowledge, Concern for Innovation, and Institutional Esprit. Many of these topics overlap substantially with some of the goals measured by the IGI and by the Gross and Grambsch survey. In those instances, despite different items and different forms of response, the results from the IFI are highly congruent with those from the other goals inventories. For example, with respect to the scale measuring Freedom, the highest scores come from faculty responses at the private universities. The same is true with respect to the scale on Concern for Advancing Knowledge. The highest scores on Concern for Undergraduate Learning come from the private liberal arts colleges.

The two scales which, in my judgment, reflect most directly the initial intent of the IFI are Self-Study and Planning and Concern for Innovation. On those two scales the differences in mean scores at private liberal arts colleges, private universities, and public universities are relatively slight. Those in the fourth category, namely state four-year colleges, have somewhat lower scores. The institutional score for Self-Study and Planning seems to have little or no relationship to a variety of other institutional characteristics, such as the selectivity of the student body, the adequacy of the library, the faculty-student ratio, or faculty salaries. In contrast, the scale Concern for Innovation does have some positive relationship with income per student, the proportion of faculty members with doctorates, and average faculty salaries. There is a network of positive and significant connections among four of the IFI scales, namely Self-Study and Planning, Concern for Innovation, Democratic Governance, and Institutional Esprit. It would be valuable, I think, for someone to combine those four scales in a single index of institutional vitality and adaptiveness and then to examine in some detail, through case studies, institutions which score very high and very low on that composite index.

Comparative Studies of the College Environment. An instrument called the College and University Environment Scales, CUES (Pace, 1963, 1969), has been used in a thousand or so colleges and universities across the country during the past fifteen years. Its aim is to characterize the atmosphere or the educational and psychological climate of the college campus. Its method is to ask people who live in the environment to report what is generally true or not true about it. Its format is a series of statements about college life— the features and facilities of the campus, rules and regulations, the faculty, curricula, instruction and examinations, student life, extracurricular organizations, cultural events, academic demands, and other elements. Its results come from the responses of students to these statements. The instrument, then, is a device for obtaining a description of the college from the students themselves, who presumably know what the environment is like because they live in it and are part of it and who have been there long enough to have some reasonable base of observation and experience. No statement is regarded as characteristic of a college unless students agree that it is so by a margin of two to one or greater.

From a variety of preliminary studies it had been determined that college environments differed from one another primarily along five major dimensions. These dimensions, or scales, constitute the structure of CUES. The five dimensions are briefly described as follows:

1. Scholarship. The items in this scale describe an environment characterized by intellectuality and scholastic discipline. There is an emphasis on competitively high academic achievement and a serious interest in scholarship. Intellectual speculation and interest in ideas, knowledge for its own sake, and intellectual discipline are all characteristic of an environment which has a high score on the scholarship scale.

2. Awareness. The items in this scale reflect concern about and emphasis on three sorts of meaning—personal, poetic, and political. A campus with a high Awareness score reveals an emphasis on self-understanding, reflectiveness, and identity, suggesting a search for personal meaning. One would also find a wide range of opportunities and considerable student interest in creative and appreciative relationships to painting, music, drama, poetry, sculpture, and the like. There is, moreover, a concern about events around the world, and the present and future condition of humanity, suggesting a search for political meaning and idealistic commitment. In short, this campus stresses awareness of self, of society, and of esthetic stimuli. Accompanying these are an encouragement of questioning and dissent and a tolerance of nonconformity.

3. Community. The items in this scale describe a friendly, cohesive, group-oriented campus. The congenial atmosphere gives a feeling of group welfare and group loyalty. The faculty members know the students, are interested in their problems, and go out of their way to be helpful. Student life is characterized by sharing and togetherness rather than by privacy or cool detachment.

4. Propriety. The items in this scale describe an environment that is polite and considerate. Group standards of decorum are important. In general, the campus atmosphere is mannerly, considerate, proper, and conventional.

5. Practicality. The items that contribute to the score for

this scale describe an environment characterized by enterprise, organization, material benefits, and social activities. Both vocational and collegiate emphases are evident. A kind of orderly supervision is apparent in the administration and the classwork. As in many organized societies, some personal benefit and prestige can be obtained by operating in the system—knowing the right people, being in the right clubs, becoming a leader, and so forth.

In the first edition of CUES each of these scales consisted of thirty statements. In the second edition each scale consisted of twenty statements. In both the first and second editions, 100 items have been in common.

In the Technical Manual for the second edition of CUES (Pace, 1969) the scores of a group of 100 colleges and universities are reported. Their scores fall into several fairly distinctive patterns. One pattern consists of institutions having very high scores on Scholarship and Awareness and very low scores on Community, Propriety, and Practicality. This environmental profile is characteristic of highly selective universities, both public and private. These, incidentally, are institutions which, in the Carnegie classification system, would be identified as research universities. Another distinctive profile is one that also consists of very high scores on Scholarship and Awareness and very low scores on Practicality, but scores that are above average on both Community and Propriety. That pattern describes academically selective liberal arts colleges, private and nonsectarian. A third pattern is characteristic of general universities. This is a classification that excludes both the highly selective institutions and the state colleges and regional universities or other universities that do not offer a doctorate. These institutions typically have about average scores on the Scholarship scale, above average scores on Awareness, relatively low scores on Community and Propriety, and rather high scores on the Practicality dimension. The state colleges and regional universities are similar to the general universities in having equally high scores on Practicality and equally low scores on Community, but they differ from the general universities in having substantially lower scores on the Scholarship and Awareness scales. There are two other categories of liberal arts colleges. One consists of strongly denominational schools. What is most characteristic of them is their very high scores on both Community and

Propriety. The other liberal arts colleges, some of which may also be denominational but not as strongly so, also have high scores on the Community scale, but lower scores on Propriety and Practicality. These results are obviously congruent with what I have previously reported about institutional goals.

Because the way in which institutions were classified in the studies of institutional goals is not quite the same as the environmental typology based exclusively on CUES scores, my colleagues and I have reexamined our CUES data and reorganized the results so that direct comparisons can be made. We took the CUES scores from the most recent administration at 247 institutions and then classified those institutions according to the Carnegie system. We had 17 research universities, 20 doctorate-granting universities, 87 comprehensive universities and colleges, 45 selective liberal arts colleges, and 78 other liberal arts collegees. Taking an average for each of these five types of institutions, we find, as one would surely expect, that the highest average scores on the Scholarship scale come from the selective liberal arts colleges and the research universities. The highest scores on the Awareness scale also come from the selective liberal arts colleges and the research universities. On the Community scale the highest scores are clearly in the liberal arts colleges, whether selective or otherwise; the research universities have the lowest average scores. On the Practicality scale, the highest scores come from the comprehensive universities and colleges, the lowest scores from the selective liberal arts colleges, and the next lowest from the research universities. There is another scale in CUES, which was made by putting together items from some of the other scales having to do with the quality of teaching and faculty-student relationships. On that scale the highest scores come from the liberal arts colleges, followed by the comprehensive universities and colleges, and then by the research universities. These CUES scores are also compatible with the goal emphases at these different types of institutions.

New Data and New Directions for Comparative Studies. From the separate and independent studies of institutional goals, characteristics, and environments, we have seen that colleges and universities differ from one another in all three of those respects. Not all institutions assign the same priority to institutional goals. Some emphasize the goals of research and advanced scholarship;

others emphasize the goals of vocational preparation and meeting local needs; and still others emphasize goals related to students' personality development and attitudes and values. Moreover, there are other institutional characteristics associated with different patterns of goal emphasis. It makes a difference whether an institution is large or small, public or private, sectarian or nonsectarian. It makes a difference how much money is spent on instruction and on the library, and how many graduate students there are, and what proportion of the students major in arts and sciences as compared with vocational fields such as engineering, business, or education. It makes a difference whether internal or external voices have the greater influence in determining the institution's goals and priorities.

Granted that there are differences in the aims and organizational characteristics of institutions, the crucial question is whether these differences can be related to achievement by colleges and universities. To what extent do institutions achieve what they aim to achieve? From the four lines of inquiry I have briefly described— Gross and Grambsch, IGI, IFI, and CUES—it is possible to identify some connections with institutional achievement. In the Gross and Grambsch study, for example, one index of achievement was specifically reported. That was the extent to which the faculty was highly productive in research and scholarship. Faculty productivity was definitely associated with the extent to which certain types of institutional goals were strongly emphasized. These included such goals as cultivating students' intellect, developing students' objectivity, training students for scholarships and research, carrying on pure research, disseminating new ideas, encouraging graduate work, rewarding faculty members for their contributions to their profession or discipline, accepting good students only, and protecting students' right of inquiry. These goals were more likely to be stressed in private universities than in public universities, where greater importance was attached to such aims as satisfying area needs and emphasizing undergraduate instruction. Moreover, institutions that have achieved a high volume of contract research are also more likely to be ones where internal sources of influence on the institution's goals were stronger than external sources. The same connections would also hold for research universities, both public and private, in the Carnegie classification system. Also, from the Institutional Goals Inventory, data comparing the University of California with the California State Universities and Colleges and other California institutions again clearly follow this pattern.

Other evidence of institutional achievement can be drawn from the results of using the College and University Environment Scales. For example, obtaining a high score on the scales measuring Scholarship and Awareness can be regarded as an institutional achievement. If the institution aims to create an intellectual and scholarly environment, then the fact that students perceive the environment to have those characteristics is an indication of the institution's success. We know that research universities emphasize intellectual and scholarly goals. We also know that research universities have typically high scores on the Scholarship scale.

We have recently assembled some new data showing how scores on the College and University Environmental Scales are related to other institutional characteristics and to more direct measures of student achievement. On the basis of CUES data from the 247 colleges and universities I previously identified, we found, for example, that the scholarship emphasis in the environment was generally accompanied by a parallel emphasis on awareness, by the academic selectivity of the student body, by the amount of money spent on education and specifically on instruction and on the library, and by a greater programmatic emphasis on the academic disciplines than on vocational or professional programs.

We need not limit ourselves, however, to the successful creation of a particular type of environment as a measure of institutional achievement. In the previous section on alumni studies I reported the results of a survey conducted at UCLA, involving seventy-four colleges and universities, which included a list of objectives that might be achieved by graduates in greater or lesser degree. At the same time the alumni survey was made, in 1969, my colleagues and I also made a parallel survey of upperclassmen. The questionnaire to upperclassmen included the same list of educational objectives. The instructions were as follows: "In thinking over your experience in college up to now, to what extent do you feel you have made progress or been benefited in each of the following respects?" To each of the objectives the students could respond by checking "very much," "quite a bit," "some," or "very little." In addition, the questionnaire included an abbreviated version of the College and

University Environment Scales. This consisted of four statements about each of the five dimensions measured by CUES. The statements were selected to be reasonably representative of the content of the full-length scales and also to produce a score that would correlate substantially with the score obtained from the complete version of CUES. We have, then, for sixty-seven colleges and universities, not only their scores on the abbreviated version of CUES but also, from a cross-section of their upperclassmen, an estimate of progress toward the attainment of important objectives. (The colleges of engineering and science were eliminated because of their specialization.) From our files of CUES data we found that thirty of these sixty-seven institutions had at some time before or after the upperclassmen survey also administered the full-length version of CUES to a sample of their students. Using these two sets of data, one for sixty-seven institutions with the short form of CUES and one for thirty of the same institutions with the long form of CUES, we computed correlations between CUES scores and students' self-estimated progress toward the attainment of various objectives. Rather than report both sets of correlations, or choosing one set over the other, I have elected to strike a balance between the two in the belief that this composite estimate of relationships would be a fairer indication of their magnitude. These data add another link to the chain of connections among institutional goals, other institutional characteristics, institutional environment, and now student achievement.

What student achievements are related to the institution's score on the Scholarship scale? Students' progress toward the following objectives is positively and significantly related to the Scholarship dimension of CUES:

- "Background and specialization for further education in some professional, scientific, or scholarly field" (.47)
- "Broadened literary acquaintance and appreciation" (.50)
- "Awareness of different philosophies, cultures, and ways of life" (.49)
- "Critical thinking—logic, inference, nature and limitations of knowledge" (.31)
- "Esthetic sensitivity—appreciation and enjoyment of art, music, drama" (.30)
- "Science and technology—understanding and appreciation" (.36)

- "Appreciation of individuality and independence of thought and action" (.38)

     With the Awareness dimension of the environment, the following student outcomes are correlated positively and significantly:

- "Broadened literary acquaintance and appreciation" (.44)
- "Awareness of different philosophies, cultures, and ways of life" (.53)
- "Critical thinking" (.33)
- "Esthetic sensitivity" (.34)
- "Appreciation of individuality and independence" (.42)
- "Personal development—understanding one's abilities and limitations, interests and standards of behavior" (.38)

     With respect to what is measured by the Community dimension on CUES, we know that the private liberal arts colleges are the ones that attach the greatest importance to goals related to that concept. We also know that these colleges have the highest scores on the CUES Community scale. Student attainments correlating positively and significantly with environments characterized by a sense of community, supportiveness, and loyalty are the following:

- "Social development—experience and skill in relating to other people" (.30)
- "Appreciation of individuality and independence of thought and action" (.30)
- "Tolerance and understanding of other people and their values" (.36)
- "Development of friendships and loyalties of lasting value" (.66)

     The Practicality dimension of CUES, which characterizes an environment having bureaucratic, entrepreneurial, status-oriented, and pragmatic features, correlates positively and significantly with the following two student attainments:

- "Vocational training—skills and techniques directly applicable to a job" (.64)
- "Bases for improved social and economic status" (.71)

The institutions having high scores on practicality are the state colleges and regional universities, the four-year state colleges, and the community colleges. These are also the institutions that attribute greatest importance to the goals of vocational training and serving local needs.

The links among institutional goals, organization, environment, and achievement are not complete. The connections I have tried to piece together are, for the most part, based on the general consistency of the results from different inventories that have some overlapping content, and from different groups of institutions that have used one or more of those inventories, and from a relatively few indicators of institutional achievement. There are indeed broad patterns of congruence and differentiation. We have seen that institutions which place great importance on research and scholarly goals are ones in which a high level of faculty research productivity has been achieved. We have seen that institutions are generally successful in creating the kind of psychological and educational climate they aim to create. And we have seen that students report progress toward objectives that are congruent with the institution's environmental emphasis and aims.

Nevertheless, these connecting links between goals and achievements could and should be more securely documented. Although the main line or central tendency of the associations reported here would very likely be confirmed by such documentation efforts, we could write and speak more confidently and persuasively about those connections if our data base were more comprehensive and unified. So, a major new direction in the study of institutions should be to assemble a stronger comparative data base from which to draw conclusions about the connections among goals, organization, environment, and achievement.

Possibly a significant step in this direction could be taken without collecting any new data. That would depend on how many colleges and universities have in fact used each of several inventories and measuring instruments. Over the past ten to fifteen years an array of inventories, questionnaires, and achievement tests have been produced or distributed by the Educational Testing Service, and since the results have been processed by ETS, they presumably exist on computer tapes at ETS. These instruments have included the College Student Questionnaire, the Institutional Goals Inventory, the Institutional Functioning Inventory, the College and University Environment Scales, and the Area and Field Tests of the Undergraduate Assessment Program. More than 1300 institutions have used one or more of these instruments.

Since the chain of connections to be analyzed begins with the institution's goals, the first question to be answered is, How many colleges and universities have used the Institutional Goals Inventory? In the California study alone there were more than 100 institutions, and during the years 1972–1975 the IGI was used by about 150 other institutions, and presumably by still more since then. The first link in the chain might be as many as 400 colleges and universities. The second question is, how many of those institutions have also used the College and University Environment Scales? We know that CUES results from several hundred institutions are on tape at UCLA, if not at ETS. The third question is, How many of these common institutions have also used the Area and/or Field Tests of the Undergraduate Assessment Program? We know that about 300 used the UAP measures in 1976–1978, that 200 or so used them in 1969–1971, and that still others used them in between.

If it turned out that IGI, and CUES, and UAP results were available for only a handful of institutions, then there would be little point in pursuing the matter further. If, however, such common data exist for, say, at least 100 to 200 institutions, and if those institutions represent a reasonable diversity of colleges and universities, then it would be worthwhile to merge the data for comparative analyses and to add other important information to them. From the government's Higher Education General Information Survey (HEGIS), one could add much information about the organization —size, form of control, degrees offered, proportion of students majoring in different fields, proportion of graduate students, education and general expenditures, instructional expenditure per student, per-student expenditure on the library, volume of contract research, and so on. One could also add the average SAT score of entering freshmen or some other index of selectivity. All these additional items of information would be available for all the institutions. Then, with a common set of institutions and a common set of information about them, one could explore more rigorously the connections between goals, organizational characteristics, environments, and outcomes.

There may be other existing data sets that could be collated. Each year several hundred colleges and universities participate in the survey of entering freshmen directed by Alexander Astin. Many of those institutions may also have used the Institutional Goals Inventory and some of the other instruments I have mentioned. That would add still another important link for subsequent analysis. The chief weakness in all these available data, however, is the limited number of measures of institutional achievement. Students' scores on standardized achievement tests are relevant criterion measures for some institutional goals. But there are many others for which comparably well-developed criteria are lacking—for goals such as the dissemination of new ideas, public service, cultural leadership in the community, and the advancement of knowledge. Despite the gaps, valuable insight could surely be gained by concerted efforts to synthesize the information that currently exists. Beyond seeking to capitalize on what we already have, we should place new, large-scale comparative studies high on the research agenda for the future specifically, studies that consider a variety of institutional achievements and in turn relate those achievements to institutional goals, organizational characteristics, and other variables.

Epilogue

In the preceding essays, or sections, I have looked at achievement testing, alumni surveys, and studies of institutions, noting highlights of what has been done and learned over the past fifty years or so and in each case proposing new directions for inquiry in the years ahead. Here, then, is a brief summary of what I saw in the past and what I would like to see in the future.

From the past use of achievement tests measuring students' knowledge and understanding of the most common fields of study in college—the sciences, social sciences, and humanities—we know that undergraduates acquire knowledge about a lot of subjects. The more they study a subject, the more they know about it. They know most about subjects that are most closely related to their major field; but their knowledge in other fields also increases. Seniors know more than sophomores; juniors know more than freshmen. These results were fully documented in the early 1930s in the Pennsylvania study. The same pattern of results was confirmed in the 1940s with the Tests of General Education. The results were reconfirmed in the 1950s with the Area Tests and the Field Tests of the Graduate Record Examinations. In the 1960s and 1970s the measures used for the College Level Examination Program, and for ETS's Under-

166

graduate Assessment Program, have yielded similar conclusions. Thus there is a basic consistency in the results from achievement testing over a span of fifty years.

For the future there are two new directions that need to be taken. First, we need to make better use of the good measures we now have. The tests of general education, now typically given to seniors, should also be given to freshmen, sophomores, and juniors. This has been done in the past, but the samples have not been comparable. Moreover, except for some of the early testing programs in the 1930s to the 1950s, there are no nationally reported results from giving the same tests to the same students at different times. Good cross-sectional studies permit valid inferences about students' growth in knowledge. Longitudinal studies provide direct evidence of that growth. We will strengthen our understanding of learning during the college years if we will make fuller use of our existing measures.

The second new direction for achievement testing should be to expand the variety of measures than can be used. Over the past several decades the nationally used achievement tests have been broadly similar in content, measuring knowledge and comprehension of basic materials in science, social science, and humanities. Our judgments about what students learn in college are necessarily limited by what sort of learning we decide to measure. We need to broaden the base of our judgments. At ACT, the staff is developing measures whose content is drawn from practical adult situations. At ETS, measures are being developed that focus on basic intellectual competence and processes—in communication, analytic thinking, synthesizing ability, and awareness of the implications, values, and social contexts of ideas and actions. I have suggested three other lines of development: tests to measure students' acquaintance with significant concepts and theories in a variety of specializations; tests to measure students' understanding and maturity in thinking about major ideas and values, such as justice, liberty, equality, and freedom; and tests to measure the integration of knowledge, values, and action within the individual. For the future, then, we need to extend our use of achievement tests and to expand the range and variety of achievement measures.

With respect to college graduates, we know from past alumni surveys over a period of forty years that they typically have good jobs and good incomes, like their jobs, think their college experience was relevant and useful in their work, look back on their college years with considerable satisfaction, participate to a considerable extent in a variety of civic and cultural activities, and believe that college contributed to their breadth of knowledge, interpersonal skills, values, and critical thinking. We also know from these alumni surveys that the patterns of their activities and interests as adults, and the particular benefits which they attribute to their college experience, are generally parallel to the patterns of emphasis of their major field curriculum and the environment of the college they attended. We also know, from national sample surveys of adults over two decades, that college graduates as a group, of all ages and in all periods, more frequently possess knowledge about public affairs, people in the news, geography, history, humanities, sciences, and popular culture than do adults who had lesser amounts of schooling.

For the future, the most useful new direction for alumni studies would, in my view, be an effort to bring some coherence and structure to the content of alumni questionnaires. No alumni questionnaire in past surveys has ever been used more than once. We do not have a battery of measures, each tapping an important and widely recognized dimension of life after college. That the results of alumni surveys have been generally consistent over time, despite differences in the questionnaires, the samples of institutions, and the ages of the alumni, is all the more remarkable. I believe the time is ripe to construct some standardized inquiry forms. Instead of hoping to find some uniformity in a diversity of separate inquiries, we should try to build some basic uniformity from which subsequent diversity could branch out, as may be desirable in special situations. Such a common core should include measures of knowledge, of occupational and personal satisfactions, of intellectual interests and habits, of the extent and quality of involvement in civic and cultural affairs, of attitudes and values and perspectives, of views about their own higher education and about higher education as a major social institution, and of their experience in graduate and professional education as well as their undergraduate experience.

Some of my colleagues would argue that the main line of evidence I have presented from past studies about the learning of undergraduates and the subsequent interests and attainments of alumni does not necessarily mean that these attainments were caused solely by the college exposure and that they might not, at least to some extent, be explained equally well or better by other factors, such as family background or SAT scores. My own view, however, is that one cannot separate education from all other experience or conditions in some cause-and-effect relationship. For the person experiencing it, college is part of a cumulative life history. Moreover, family background, SAT score, and similar conditions cannot be regarded as causes of learning. They can only be regarded as factors that may be related to greater or lesser amounts of learning, given the basic conditions for learning in the first place. You can put a person with an I.Q. of 180 on a deserted island for a year without any books, and he will learn nothing about Shakespeare. You can put him in college, and in a Shakespeare class, and he may indeed learn more than a student with an I.Q. of 100; but neither will learn anything without exposure to the material. Basically, what students learn depends on what they study. They are selective consumers of what is available to them, their selectivity being influenced by their interests and aspirations. And seldom are those interests and aspirations totally opposite from what has emerged during eighteen years or so of previous developmental history. While college serves to expand knowledge and interests, it also serves to strengthen and deepen them. The general direction of that development in college can still be observed in the activities and interests of college graduates five, ten, and twenty years later. Given the concept of college impress, that adds up to quite an impression.

Whether the results of research over the next several decades will add up to the same conclusions remains to be seen. We can be sure, however, that new studies will not lead to contrary conclusions. We will not suddenly discover that people who study least know the most, or that seniors know less than freshmen about the subjects taught in college. Nor will we find that college graduates are, on the average, more ignorant of current events than nongraduates, or read less, or less frequently attend concerts or plays or visit galleries. Nor will we find that college graduates are no longer employed in jobs that require knowledge, judgment, perspective, critical thinking, and effective communication. Nevertheless there are conditions that could modify some of our conclusions. As a greater proportion of young people go to college, the relative difference between those who do and the total age group will necessarily be somewhat less. That is already evident with respect to income. To the extent that future studies compare persons who have benefited from all forms of postsecondary education against the total age group, the relative differences will also be less. But if future studies, like past studies, consider only those who get bachelor's and higher degrees, the differences will probably remain. The community colleges and the proprietary schools serve a different clientele, have a different curriculum, and serve different purposes. They should, in my opinion, be studied separately, and on their own terms, if their achievements are to be properly assessed.

As for the achievements of institutions, we have looked at two main sources of data or two approaches to getting evidence: self-studies and institutional research, and external, comparative studies. Objective, data-based inquiries to evaluate internal programs and practices were numerous in the decades of the 1930s to the 1950s at such places as Minnesota, Purdue, Illinois, Michigan State, and Chicago. These analyses were typically concerned with the prediction of students' success, the study of retention and drop out, the comparison of different teaching methods, the evaluation of curricula, students' evaluation of teaching, faculty load, student attitudes and satisfactions, orientation programs, remedial programs, extracurricular activities, and so on. Such studies gradually came to be called institutional research. Institutional research offices now exist in most universities and many colleges; but the focus of their activity has shifted from educational evaluation to institutional accounting, emphasizing the collection of information about instructional costs, space utilization, and similar topics of concern to budget makers.

Meanwhile, mainly following World War II, self-studies became common. Self-studies typically were concerned with the educational goals of the college, with the educational programs of the college, with recommendations for clarification and improvement, and, in the conduct of self-studies, with the cooperation and involvement of the faculty. No major generalizations have emerged from the results of self-studies, primarily because the reports are usually internal documents not published for a wider audience. From the experience of self-studies, however, there has emerged considerable agreement about the desirable scope and the procedures for undertaking them, as well as agreement that self-studies are a worthwhile activity. The fact that self-studies have now been firmly connected with the accreditation process means that they will continue to be made. It also means that any improvements in the concept of self-study, and the methods and data base employed, should find a receptive audience.

For the future, self-studies run the risk of being perceived as a necessary chore, periodically demanding some local time and effort, a job to get over and done with every five years or so. What may be needed is a more significant concept, the concept of an institutional case study. This may be analogous to the clinician's developmental case history or to a historian's biography. The historian seeks more than an enumeration of events and accomplishments in the subject's history. The historian examines the formative years, the influences of people and circumstances, the conditions which may have shaped character, the successes and failures along the way, the decisions, and the accomplishments of the subject. A good biography is dynamic and revealing, helping to explain how things turned out the way they did in the life and times of the character. A good institutional case study needs historical perspective, models to guide the exploration of the dynamics of institutional operations and attainment, and reliable instruments to measure the processes and the results. To this end, I described three models: first, a way to look at the dynamics of action following the Syracuse self-survey; second, a model for examining the dynamics of students' development and learning in which the quality of their effort interacts with pressures, facilities, and opportunities in the college environment; and third, a means of analyzing the effective mechanisms by which the college adapts to changing conditions.

The accomplishments of the comparative studies may be grouped in four main categories: first, the development of standard definitions essential for making interinstitutional comparisons; second, the making of recommendations for improved practices; third, the development of statewide master plans for higher education; and fourth, the creation of a nationwide base of information about higher education. Education surveys, objective and comparative in nature, have a long history, from the early part of the twentieth century to the present, and many of them brought about important changes in higher education. Flexner's survey of medical education resulted in upgrading the standards for medical schools. Surveys showing inadequate provisions for faculty retirement income resulted in the creation of the Teachers Insurance Annuity Association. Surveys in connection with President Truman's Commission on Higher Education resulted in reducing economic, racial, and religious barriers to college admission, in the expansion of junior colleges, and in a much greater federal investment in financial aid to students. The surveys made for the Carnegie Commission on Higher Education extended our knowledge about different types of institutions and about emergent problems faced by the colleges and universities. The National Center for Educational Statistics, which now annually collects census-type information about all colleges and universities, has become an essential data source for comparative analyses and for understanding the complexity of higher education in the U.S.

All these surveys have produced a vast amount of data about the conditions of higher education, but they have not produced, nor were they in most cases primarily intended to produce, knowledge about the achievement or effectiveness of institutions. More recent comparative studies, using standardized survey instruments such as the Institutional Goals Inventory, the Institutional Functioning Inventory, and the College and University Environment Scales, have now given us at least some basis for studying institutional effectiveness. We know, for example, that institutions that place great importance on such goals as research, scholarship, and advanced training are generally successful in achieving those goals, as evidenced by faculty research productivity, the volume of contract research, the production of Ph.D.s, and the development of a campus atmosphere that is perceived by students to have a strong scholarly emphasis. There are also other generally congruent relationships between goals and attainments, including evidence that students' self-estimates of progress toward various goals are greatest with respect to the type of goals emphasized by the institution.

For the future, if we are to learn more about the connections

between institutional goals, characteristics, environments, and outcomes, we will need to put together information from all these
sources—from HEGIS, from goals inventories, from environmental
studies, and from research on other aspects of institutional functioning—in new, large-scale comparative studies. We will also need
achievement or outcome measures of sufficient scope to match
the diversity of institutional purposes.

Knowledge for New Insight

In the section on "Achievement During College," I deliber-
ately focused on the results from standardized achievement tests. I
did so because these kinds of data, and especially the results from
such testing over a period of several decades, have not previously
been pulled together and highlighted in one place. I also concentrated on achievement tests because I believe that the acquisition of
knowledge is the primary, and certainly the most obvious, aim of
college courses and curricula. Professors seek to impart knowledge
of facts and principles, of generalizations and concepts, of ways of
thinking about phenomena, of interpretations of data and meanings,
of underlying assumptions, and similar information and processes
related to the subject matter of their courses. It is this kind of
knowledge and intellectual development that makers of achievement
tests have sought to measure. I would not want anyone to infer,
however, that I regard other lines of student development in college
as less important. The college influence on students' attitudes, interests, aspirations, values, and personal traits is equally significant.
Indeed, its effect on personal development has been emphasized and
well documented in the research literature, and it is only because
of that thorough documentation that I have not dealt with it in my
own section on achievement during college.

What needs to be done in future research is to examine the
ways in which knowledge and personal development interact. For
the most part, researchers who have studied personality development
during the college years and after, or who have measured changes
in students' attitudes and values, have done just that and no more.
And researchers who have studied students' acquisition of knowledge and intellectual skills have done just that and no more. Each

by itself is a major topic of inquiry. But we need to know more than we now know about how they fit together. Some psychologists would argue that personality traits such as nonauthoritarianism, flexibility, tolerance of ambiguity, curiosity, openness to change, and one's sense of personal identity, self-confidence, and self-esteem are necessary prerequisites of the absorption of new knowledge in the larger personality. Other psychologists would assert that the successful acquisition of knowledge, understanding, and intellectual skills leads to or helps to produce self-confidence, self-esteem, openness to further experience, and similar personality traits.

Despite the growing numbers of older students, part-time students, and commuting students, the college experience for most people begins in the late teens and involves living on the campus. About 95 percent of first-time, full-time college freshmen who enter universities or four-year colleges are young people who graduated from high school in June and started college in September. About 95 percent of them are nineteen years old or younger. And from two thirds to three fourths of them begin their college experience by living in a dormitory, fraternity/sorority, or other college housing. The opportunities for out-of-class experiences leading to personal and social development are extensive. Indeed, if one assumes that the typical freshman student spends about fifteen hours a week in class, and another twenty to thirty hours a week in study and other academically related activities, he or she still has about eight hours a day, not counting weekends, for an assortment of personal and social activities. With time divided more or less equally between academic and nonacademic activities, the opportunity for studying their interaction is ideal.

Although large-scale comparative studies might throw some light on these interactions, it seems much more likely to me that on-campus case studies, combining clinical interviews, observations, and paper-and-pencil inventories and tests, will generate more thorough understanding. So, one type of knowledge for new insight could come from exploring how academic development and other lines of personal development may reinforce one another.

A second type of knowledge for new insight is what I will call knowledge for institutional stability. Paradoxical as it may seem, this knowledge consists mainly of knowledge about institutional adaptiveness and change. The adaptive mechanisms or capacity of colleges and universities may be analogous to the stabilizer on an ocean liner, enabling the ship to ride more smoothly and safely through the turbulent waves and currents around it. Stability comes from responding to the waves. In colleges and universities the capacity for responsiveness depends on knowledge, on awareness of events and conditions in the surrounding society. All offices within the institution having significant connections with people and events outside the institution need to share their information and periodically assess its import. The chief administrator, the trustees, the alumni office, the people who deal with recruitment and admissions, the development office, the planning office, the institutional research office, the placement office—all these individuals or groups have outside contacts by the very nature of their positions. And, of course, appropriate faculty committees must be privy to this information and join significantly in discussing what it means, because new programs, new services, revised curricula and requirements, and many other changes both large and small require action by the faculty. Remember David Henry's observation that one of the characteristics of higher education over the past several decades has been "the constancy of change." Stability is maintained by successfully adapting to change.

There is another side to the paradox of stability through change. When psychologists speak of a mature person or a well-developed personality, they usually mean one who has a clear sense of identity, a self-concept rooted in experience and reality, and a record of achievement, and as a result, one who is open to new ideas and new experiences. So, too, colleges and universities with a clear sense of their identity and mission and with a realistic assessment of their developmental history and accomplishments are, or should be, in the best position to make creative responses to changing circumstances. Too often, when confronted by crises or threats, administrators tighten controls. This is a mistake. Channels of communication need to be opened and widened, not closed and narrowed. Creativity is stimulated by freedom, not by restrictions.

In making judgments about the achievement of institutions and about the achievement of their students and alumni, one must give due honor and respect to the diversity of higher education in the United States. I have shown that institutions differ in their aims, their environments, and their accomplishments. Moreover, their aims, their sense of mission and identity, are recognized and given priority with considerable agreement among the people in the institutions. We cannot say that Minnesota is better or worse than DePauw, any more than we can say that a ping-pong player is better or worse than a polo player. Minnesota and DePauw are not playing the same game. It is true, of course, that all colleges and universities, albeit with varying degrees of emphasis and in different ways, are engaged in undergraduate instruction. But I often think we do a disservice to ourselves and to the public whenever we evaluate institutions against a single criterion, concluding inevitably that half of them are below average. We blur their individuality; we diminish the public's ability to understand and appreciate differences; we push them to be like others rather than to do better what they aim to do; and perhaps thereby we undermine the stability, identity, and past achievements which may well be a necessary base for responding creatively and uniquely to whatever their particular problems or opportunities may be. When we do undertake national evaluations of higher education, we need to employ a range of critera that matches the range of institutional goals. And we need to report our results in ways that pay proper regard to the fact that we have a diverse system of higher education, not one system of higher education.

There is a third kind of knowledge that can contribute to institutional stability and adaptiveness—namely, knowledge about public attitudes. High school students, college students, former students, parents, taxpayers, employers, racial and ethnic minorities, people in business and labor, in the professions, and in all other parts of society are the public. What do they think about higher education? We have pretty good answers to that question from college students and alumni, but not from the general public. Much of what the public hears and reads about higher education comes from newspaper stories, anecdotes told by friends and acquaintances, perhaps a magazine article or a TV program. Usually the information is about something unusual—cheating at West Point, the Ph.D. working in the gas station, the superstars of college sports, a lawsuit, or whatever else might catch the eye of the reader or the ear of the listener. Those of us in the colleges and universities are told that public attitudes are this or that as the case may be, but the source of that information is someone's impression. The source is rarely a well-designed, scientifically selected sample survey of public opinion. We need such surveys, regularly and on a broad range of topics.

How does the public value higher education? What do our citizens think colleges and universities are for? Do they think knowledge and understanding are inherently valuable, or valuable only if they pay off in the market place? Do they think intellectual and cultural benefits are as important as economic benefits, perhaps even more important? Do they think most students waste their time, gain little benefit of any sort, and are simply in college because there is nothing else to do? If they think too many people are going to college, which people would they exclude? Do they think any student should be entitled to go to any school? Do they think colleges and universities are run inefficiently and wastefully? Do they think "college professor" is an occupation of high prestige? What importance do they attach to science, philosophy, history, literature, and other major categories of knowledge? Do they think that being a college graduate is an important and valuable asset for senators and representatives, cabinet officers and diplomats, and heads of major corporations, or that it doesn't matter? What segments of the public attach the most or the least importance to higher education, and to what aspects of higher education?

We do know something about public attitudes; and what we know appears to be very positive and supportive. A California poll (Field Research Corporation, 1978) conducted in February 1978 revealed that universities and colleges rank high in public confidence —higher than banks and financial institutions, higher than the U.S. Supreme Court, higher than the medical profession, higher than organized religion, higher than manufacturing corporations, higher than the public school system, higher than the national Congress. Only research scientists ranked higher than universities and colleges. Many research scientists are in universities. Forty-three percent said they had "a lot of confidence" in universities and colleges. This figure compares with 49 percent for research scientists, 35 percent for the medical profession, and 14 percent for the national Congress.

When the responses "a lot of confidence" and "some confidence" are combined, the resulting figures were 85 percent for research scientists, 84 percent for universities and colleges, 80 percent for the U.S. Supreme Court, 76 percent for the medical profession, and 70 percent for the national Congress.

Perhaps colleges and universities should establish a higher education opinion-polling agency. More feasibly, they should at least contract with established agencies for periodic polls that have a well-designed population sample and use a national corps of trained interviewers. Remember David Henry's observation that among the three elements which stood out in his recollections of higher education over the past four or five decades, one was "the significance of public evaluation and the nature of public interaction."

One final note. Potential new developments in achievement testing, in studies of college graduates, and in institutional case studies give promise to enrich further our understanding of the path of student development and college impress and of the features of the institutions themselves which help to facilitate it. As to the conditions that help the college as an organization remain alert and adaptive to changing circumstances, there are models for thinking about those conditions and information relevant to them. To understand the organization and its administration more thoroughly, I think we need a model similar in intent to the model for studying student development and college impress. A major feature of that model was a set of scales for measuring the amount, scope, and quality of the effort students invest in using the resources and opportunities intended to facilitate their learning and development. What we need in the study of organizations is a set of scales for measuring the amount, nature, and quality of the administrative effort or organizational effort intended to facilitate the attainment of organizational goals. If and when we can make that connection between activities and achievement, we may be able to answer, better than we can now, the question, How do we get from here to there?

References

ASTIN, A. *Four Critical Years: Effects of College on Beliefs, Attitudes, and Knowledge.* San Francisco: Jossey-Bass, 1977.

BROWNE, A. D. "A Follow-Up and Reanalysis of the Syracuse University Self-Survey: A Study of Institutional Change." Unpublished doctoral dissertation, Syracuse University, 1952.

CALVERT, R. J., JR. *Career Patterns of Liberal Arts Graduates.* Cranston, R.I.: Carroll Press, 1969.

Carnegie Commission on Higher Education. *Digest of Reports of the Carnegie Commission on Higher Education.* New York: McGraw-Hill, 1974.

Carnegie Commission on Higher Education. *Sponsored Research of the Carnegie Commission on Higher Education.* New York: McGraw-Hill, 1975.

COHEN, M. D., and MARCH, J. G. *Leadership and Ambiguity: The American College President.* New York: McGraw-Hill, 1974.

College Entrance Examination Board. *Score Distributions: General Examinations, College-Level Examination Program, Candidates Tested Through the United States Armed Forces Institute, July 1965–December 1966.* New York: College Entrance Examination Board, 1968.

179

Commission on Higher Education of the Middle States Association of Colleges and Schools. *Handbook for Institutional Self-Study.* Philadelphia: Commission on Higher Education of the Middle States Association of Colleges and Schools, 1978.

DONALDSON, R. *Fortifying Higher Education: A Story of College Self-Studies.* New York: Fund for the Advancement of Education, 1959.

DRESSEL, P. L. (Ed.). *Evaluation in General Education.* Dubuque, Iowa: Wm. C. Brown, 1954.

DRESSEL, P. L. *Handbook of Academic Evaluation: Assessing Institutional Effectiveness, Student Progress, and Professional Performance for Decision Making in Higher Education.* San Francisco: Jossey-Bass, 1976.

ECKERT, R. *Outcomes of General Education.* Minneapolis: University of Minnesota Press, 1943.

ECKERT, R., and KELLER, R. (Eds.). *A University Looks at Its Program.* Minneapolis: University of Minnesota Press, 1954.

Educational Testing Service. *Institutional Testing Program: Summary Statistics 1953–1954.* ETS Archives Microfiche No. 40. Princeton, N.J.: Educational Testing Service, 1954.

Educational Testing Service. *Undergraduate Assessment Program Guide.* Princeton, N.J.: Educational Testing Service, 1976.

Educational Testing Service. *Undergraduate Assessment Program Guide.* Princeton, N.J.: Educational Testing Service, 1978.

EELLS, W. C. *Surveys of American Higher Education.* New York: Carnegie Foundation for the Advancement of Teaching, 1937.

EURICH, A. C., and PACE, C. R. *A Follow-Up Study of Minnesota Graduates from 1928–1936.* Minneapolis: Committee on Educational Research, University of Minnesota, 1938.

FELDMAN, K. A., and NEWCOMB, T. M. *The Impact of College on Students: An Analysis of Four Decades of Research.* San Francisco: Jossey-Bass, 1969a.

FELDMAN, K. A., and NEWCOMB, T. M. *The Impact of College on Students: Summary Tables.* San Francisco: Jossey-Bass, 1969b.

FEUERBORN, T. "Organizational Adaptation in Higher Education." Unpublished doctoral dissertation, UCLA, 1971.

Field Research Corporation. *The California Poll, February 1978.* San Francisco: Field Institute, 1978.

FLEXNER, A. *Medical Education in the United States and Canada.*

New York: Carnegie Foundation for the Advancement of Teaching, 1910.

FORREST, A. F., and STEELE, J. M. *College Outcome Measures Project.* Iowa City: American College Testing Program, 1978.

GRAUBARD, S. (Ed.). "Discoveries and Interpretations: Studies in Contemporary Scholarship." *Daedalus,* 1977a, *1* (entire issue).

GRAUBARD, S. (Ed.). "Discoveries and Interpretations: Studies in Contemporary Scholarship." *Daedalus,* 1977b, *2* (entire issue).

GREENLEAF, W. *Economic Status of College Alumni.* Bulletin 1937, No. 10. Washington, D.C.: Office of Education, U.S. Department of the Interior, 1939.

GROSS, E., and GRAMBSCH, P. V. *Changes in University Organization, 1964–1971.* New York: McGraw-Hill, 1974.

HARVEY, P., and LANNHOLM, G. "Achievement in Three Major Fields During the Last Two Years of College." *Graduate Record Examination Special Report 60-Z.* Princeton, N.J.: Educational Testing Service, 1960.

HAVEMANN, E., and WEST, P. S. *They Went to College.* New York: Harcourt Brace Jovanovich, 1952.

HAVEN, E. W. *The Sophomore Norming Sample for the General Examinations of the College-Level Examination Program.* Statistical Report SR-64-63. Princeton, N.J.: Educational Testing Service, 1964.

HENRY, D. D. *Challenges Past, Challenges Present: An Analysis of American Higher Education Since 1930.* San Francisco: Jossey-Bass, 1975.

HYMAN, H. H., WRIGHT, C. R., and REED, J. S. *The Enduring Effects of Education.* Chicago: University of Chicago Press, 1975.

KATZ, J. "Benefits for Personal Development from Going to College." Paper presented at the annual meeting of the Association for the Study of Higher Education, Chicago, March 6–7, 1976.

LANNHOLM, G. V. "Educational Growth During the Second Two Years of College." *Educational and Psychological Measurement,* 1952, *12* (4), 645–653.

LEARNED, W. S., and WOOD, B. D. *The Student and His Knowledge: A Report to the Carnegie Foundation on the Results of the High School and College Examinations of 1928, 1930, and 1932.* Bulletin No. 29. New York: Carnegie Foundation for the Advancement of Teaching, 1938.

LENNING, O., and others. *Nonintellective Correlates of Grades, Persistence, and Academic Learning in College: The Published Literature Through the Decade of the Sixties.* Iowa City: American College Testing Program, 1974a.

LENNING, O., and others. *The Many Faces of College Success and Their Nonintellective Correlates: The Published Literature Through the Decade of the Sixties.* Iowa City: American College Testing Program, 1974b.

MOOS, R. *Evaluating Educational Environments: Procedures, Measures, Findings, and Policy Implications.* San Francisco: Jossey-Bass, 1979.

National Center for Higher Education Management Systems. *Recent-Alumni Questionnaire.* Boulder, Colo.: National Center for Higher Education Management Systems, 1979.

PACE, C. R. *They Went to College.* Minneapolis: University of Minnesota Press, 1941.

PACE, C. R. *College and University Environment Scales.* Princeton, N.J.: Educational Testing Service, 1963.

PACE, C. R. *College and University Environment Scales. Second Edition: Technical Manual.* Princeton, N.J.: Educational Testing Service, 1969.

PACE, C. R. *Education and Evangelism.* New York: McGraw-Hill, 1972.

PACE, C. R. *The Demise of Diversity?* Berkeley, Calif.: Carnegie Commission on Higher Education, 1974.

PACE, C. R. *College Student Experiences.* Los Angeles: UCLA Laboratory for Research on Higher Education, 1979.

PACE, C. R., and TROYER, M. *Self-Survey: Report to the Faculty.* Syracuse, N.Y.: Syracuse University, 1949.

PETERSON, R. E. *Goals for California Higher Education: A Survey of 116 College Communities.* Sacramento: Joint Committee on the Master Plan for Higher Education, California Legislature, 1973.

PETERSON, R. E., and UHL, N. P. *Formulating College and University Goals: A Guide for Using the Institutional Goals Inventory.* Princeton, N.J.: Educational Testing Service, 1977.

PETERSON, R. E., and others. *Institutional Functioning Inventory. Preliminary Technical Manual.* Princeton, N.J.: Educational Testing Service, 1970.

President's Commission on Higher Education. *Higher Education for American Democracy.* New York: Harper & Row, 1947.

REEVES, F. W., and others. *The Liberal Arts College.* Chicago: University of Chicago Press, 1932.

RUDOLPH, F. *Curriculum: A History of the American Undergraduate Course of Study Since 1636.* San Francisco: Jossey-Bass, 1977.

SOLMON, L., BISCONTI, A., and OCHSNER, N. *College as a Training Ground for Jobs.* New York: Praeger, 1977.

SPAETH, J., and GREELEY, A. *Recent Alumni and Higher Education.* New York: McGraw-Hill, 1970.

SPAFFORD, I., and others. *Building a Curriculum for General Education.* Minneapolis: University of Minnesota Press, 1943.

STICKLER, H. *Institutional Research Concerning Land-Grant Institutions and State Universities.* Tallahassee: Florida State University Office of Institutional Research and Service, 1959.

TUNIS, J R *Was College Worthwhile?* New York: Harcourt Brace Jovanovich, 1936.

U.S. Bureau of the Census. *The Condition of Education.* Vol. 3, Pt. 1: *Statistical Report.* Washington, D.C.: U.S. Government Printing Office, 1977.

VESEY, L. *The Emergence of the American University.* Chicago: University of Chicago Press, 1965.

WALLACE, D. C. "A Description and Interpretation of the Activities and Opinions of Syracuse University Graduates Related to General Education." Unpublished doctoral dissertation, Syracuse University, 1949.

WARREN, J. "Describing College Graduates in 87 Phrases or Less." *Findings,* 1976, *3,* 5–8.

WARREN, J. *The Measurement of Academic Competence.* Berkeley, Calif.: Educational Testing Service, 1978.

WILLIAMS, C. *These We Teach.* Minneapolis: University of Minnesota Press, 1943.

WISHART, P., and ROSSMANN, J. *Career Patterns, Employment and Earnings of Graduates of 11 ACM Colleges.* Chicago: Associated Colleges of the Midwest, 1977.

ZOOK, G., and HAGGERTY, M. *Principles of Accrediting Higher Institutions.* Chicago: University of Chicago Press, 1936.

Index

184